Letts

Revise
GCSE

Physical
Education

Contents

	AQA	AQA	AQA	OCR
Syllabus name	Short Course	Full Course	Double Award	Short Course
Syllabus number	4891	4892	4894	J086
External assessment	1 test paper 45 min/40% Scenario	1 test paper 90 min/40% Scenario	2 test papers 90 min/20% 90 min/20% Scenario	1 test paper 60 min/40%
Practical performance/ Controlled Assessments	60%	60%	60%	60%
SECTION REFERENCE NUMBERS				
The major body systems	Unit 3.1 Section A	Unit 3.1 Section A		Section 3.1
Fitness	Unit 3.1 Section A	Unit 3.1 Section A		Section 3.1
Training methods and programmes	Unit 3.1 Section A	Unit 3.1 Section A		Section 3.1
Skill	Unit 3.1 Section A	Unit 3.1 Section A		Section 3.1
Measurement in sport	Unit 3.1 Section A	Unit 3.1 Section A		Section 3.1
Factors affecting performance	Unit 3.1 Section A	Unit 3.1 Section A		Section 3.1
Safety in sport	Unit 3.1 Section A	Unit 3.1 Section A		Section 3.1
Sport today	Unit 3.1 Section B	Unit 3.1 Section B		Section 3.1
Participation	Unit 3.1 Section B	Unit 3.1 Section B		Section 3.1
Media and sponsorship	Unit 3.1 Section B	Unit 3.1 Section B		
Organisation and provision of sport	Unit 3.1 Section B	Unit 3.1 Section B		Section 3.1

your GCSE course

OCR	Edexcel	Edexcel	WJEC	WJEC	CCEA
Full Course	Short Course	Long Course	Short Course	Full Course	Full Course
J586	3PE01	2PE01	266 01	197 01	7210
2 test papers 45 min/20% 60 min/20%	1 test paper 60 min/57%	1 test paper 90 min/42%	1 test paper 90 min/40%	1 test paper 90 min/40%	1 test paper 90 min/40%
60%	43%	58%	60%	60%	Controlled Assessment 20% / Practical performance 40%

SECTION REFERENCE NUMBERS

OCR	Edexcel	Edexcel	WJEC	WJEC	CCEA
Section 3.1 Section 3.3	Unit 1 1.2.1/2/3/4	Unit 1 1.2.1/2/3/4		Section B	Section 3.6
Section 3.1	Unit 1 1.2.2/3	Unit 1 1.2.2/3	Section A	Section A Section B	Section 3.1/3/6
Section 3.1 Section 3.3	Unit 1 1.1.3/4/5	Unit 1 1.1.3/4/5	Section A	Section A Section B	Section 3.4/5 Section 3.12/13
Section3.1 Section 3.3	Unit 1 1.1.4	Unit 1 1.1.4	Section A	Section A Section B	Section 3.1/10
Section 3.1			Section A	Section A	Section 3.6
Section 3.1 Section 3.3	Unit 1 1.1.2/6	Unit 1 1.1.2/6	Section A	Section A	Section 3.2/8
Section 3.1 Section 3.3	Unit 1 1.1.6 1.2.1/2	Unit 1 1.1.6 1.2.1/2	Section A	Section A	Section 3.1/2/9
Section 3.1	Unit 1 1.1.1	Unit 1 1.1.1	Section A	Section A	
Section 3.1	Unit 1 1.1.1	Unit 1 1.1.1	Section A	Section A Section B	Section 3.2/9/11
Section 3.3	Unit 1 1.1.1	Unit 1 1.1.1	Section A	Section A	
Section 3.1 Section 3.3	Unit 1 1.1.1	Unit 1 1.1.1	Section A	Section A	Section 3.11

Preparing for the examination

Although the Physical Education courses offered at GCSE level are essentially practical subjects, the **written examination is worth 40%** of the total available marks for the final grade. The exam is, therefore, a very important part of the course.

Your revision time before the exam is important. A revision programme is a big undertaking and cannot be started too early. Some careful planning and organisation, and use of this Study Guide, should pay dividends at examination time.

Preparing a revision programme

You should have covered **all the course units** to be studied. Now is the time to establish those aspects of the course that you are **least confident** about. To do this, re-try the exam practice questions (not under exam conditions) to check which parts you are a little uncertain of. Then, using this information, devise a **realistic** revision programme that will be effective. Your programme should...

- put **emphasis** on those areas that you feel you are weakest in
- **support** those areas that you feel confident in
- include a **time management** strategy.

Think of your revision programme in the same way that you would look at a simple, practical training programme. The programme should...

- be **pre-planned**
- have an **attainable** number of topics to focus on
- include a **check list**
- have **rest days** built in to it.

Each session should build on known work:

- Start with a brief **re-cap** of known work (like a warm-up session).
- Follow this with more **detailed** learning sessions on new work (like the learning of new simple skills).
- **Build up** to more concentrated practice / revision sessions (like hard, intensive training).
- Finish off with a simple **self test** session (like a cool down).

How this book can help

This Study Guide can help because...

- it covers all the **essential topics** for your scheme
- it contains **progress check** questions after every topic, and **practice questions** at the end of each unit
- it includes all the answers, together with **advice** from experienced examiners
- it contains useful **examiners' hints and tips** printed clearly in the margins
- it gives **key points** throughout, which are highlighted for emphasis.

Ways to improve your grade

Preparation is essential – the following suggestions should point you in the right direction.

Revising

When revising...

- choose a work place where you **will not** be easily distracted
- make a **realistic estimate** of what you think you can cover in one week
- **divide your time** into 30- or 40-minute sessions
- come to the revision session well-rested, and in the right **frame of mind** (ensure that you get enough sleep and are ready to work)
- choose to revise topics that you can **complete** in the set time
- use **exam-style questions** to check your learning progress
- be prepared to go back and **re-do** a topic for a second or third time if necessary, but not always in consecutive sessions.

If in doubt, ask your teachers – they are there to help!

Learning and remembering

You might want to use one or more of the following memory aids:

- **Repetition** – by writing or saying something over and over again you can often learn it 'parrot fashion'. This method has drawbacks, however, because you might remember it, but be unable to understand it.
- **Mnemonics** – the use of a word whose letters or symbols remind you of important information. For example, the **5 Ss** (which stand for strength, stamina, suppleness, speed and somatotype) relate to fitness components, and **SMART / SMARTER** relate to goal setting.
- **Flow diagrams** – make up your own. Start with a key word and link it with lines to other words in the topic you are revising. The lines may radiate outwards like a sun or go up and down like a ladder. See Chapter 11, Figure 11.3 for an example.
- **Prompt cards** – these are best made up by you, and they should contain only brief key facts or words from a specific topic. They help to jog the memory.

Preparing for the exams

The way you tackle exam questions is important. Make sure you...

- give yourself plenty of practice in **reading** exam questions – you must be able to understand what is being asked for
- **practise** answering exam questions as often as you can – this will help you to prepare for the exam and check what you have learned
- note the **mark allocation** for a particular question, or part of a question – this will indicate how many facts to give or how extensive the answer should be
- have a **positive attitude** – you know that you can do well.

Answering questions

When answering the exam questions, make sure you...

- **read** the question carefully, at least twice
- **write** clearly and legibly, and use the correct technical terms if possible
- **remember** that extra marks may be given for good spelling, punctuation and grammar
- **never** leave a blank for an answer; this never gets any marks.

Some, but not all, exam boards award extra points for good spelling, grammar and punctuation.

Controlled assessments

The Physical Education courses described in this book include **practical performances** and **controlled assessments**.

Practical performances

The practical performances for all exam boards are assessed by personal performance and the ability to show a knowledge and understanding of specific profiles / categories, including **Player / Performer**, **Organiser**, **Leader / Coach**, **Choreographer** and **Official**.

Player / Performer	Must demonstrate effective and suitable skills in various settings, and effective planning to improve performance.
Organiser	Must demonstrate the ability to promote, plan and run a specific event / competition. Written evidence of planning and preparation is required.
Leader / Coach	Must demonstrate the ability to lead, organise and coach groups, showing a knowledge of safety aspects, skills, analysis of performance and progressive learning suitable to the group being worked with.
Choreographer	Must demonstrate the ability to design, arrange and stage a specific dance performance, identify levels of performance and show how these might be progressively improved.
Official	Must demonstrate the ability to show effective and suitable skills in a number of settings. These can be as a referee, assistant referee, timekeeper, judge or starter, depending on the activity chosen.

The precise combination of practical performance profiles / categories for each exam board should be explained to you by your teacher.

Controlled assessments

The exact nature of the assessments varies from one exam board to another. Your teacher should be able to advise you of the requirements of your course.

AQA	**AQA** will publish **scenario-based topics** prior to, but in the year of, examination. For each of the courses, the pre-released scenario should be studied, as **questions** in the **exam paper** will be based on it. For the Double Award, this process will be completed **twice**. The scenario may consist of a description of the lifestyle of an individual together with their involvement in and attitude towards physical activity **OR** a description of a performer, their routine and aspirations. • For the **first type of scenario** you should be able to describe those aspects of a healthy lifestyle that are, or are not, evident in the scenario. You should show that you know what a balanced healthy lifestyle consists of, including levels of fitness (chapter 5) and how to assess them (chapter 2), diet (chapter 6), leisure and levels of exercise (chapter 8). You must also include some information on the dangers associated with an unhealthy lifestyle (chapter 7). • For the **second type of scenario** you should show that you have a knowledge of fitness (chapter 2), training, including peaking and periodisation (chapter 3), diet (chapter 6), goal-setting, motivation and arousal (chapter 4), and training methods (chapter 3).

Edexcel	**Edexcel** requires students to undertake an **Analysis of Performance** task based on one of the physical activities undertaken, possibly pre-recorded on DVD / video. This is a prolonged piece of work conducted under the guidance and assessment of the teacher. It is expected to take 9–10 hours to complete. The student must be able to show... – a full knowledge of the rules and terminology of the activity – an ability to observe and analyse a specific performance in the activity – an ability to evaluate the performance, to identify strengths and weaknesses – an ability to say how identified weaknesses might be improved – an ability to plan a PEP to improve fitness and performance. The last component **must be** presented in written form and this suggests that it might be best to produce all except the first task in this manner. The first task could be completed in a question and answer session with your teacher. If a **copy** of a specific skill / performance is on DVD it can be re-run time and again in order to analyse it thoroughly. The most appropriate type of performance to analyse would be a complex, self-paced closed skill, such as the high jump. It is possible to break the whole of this performance into **discrete parts** (such as the run up, the take-off, the flight over the bar, and the arm action) and describe how each is affecting the performance as a whole. There is also an end product (i.e. the height jumped) to improve upon. A programme can be devised to improve each of these parts and should form the basis for your PEP. Do not forget the influence of the 5 Ss of fitness already studied (chapter 2), and mention any noted improvement, before and after testing (chapter 5). A simple, concise written submission is best.
OCR	**OCR** requires **two** tasks to be assessed: **1** An **Analysis of Lifestyle (AL)** to be completed within 7 hours. In the first hour, the task will be explained to you by your teacher. The next 4 hours are for you to complete your research of the topic. The last 2 hours are for you to write up your research (under the supervision of your teacher). **Three aspects** must be described: – What a balanced healthy lifestyle consists of, i.e. levels of fitness (chapter 2) and how to assess them (chapter 5), diet (chapter 6), leisure and levels of exercise (chapter 8). You must describe the dangers associated with an unhealthy lifestyle (chapter 7). – Data collected relating to the completed research. – An analysis of this data with a recommendation of how to improve on the weaknesses. **2** An **Analysis of Performance (AP)** also to be completed in 7 hours (the breakdown the same as for the first task). In the **first part** of this task, students must observe a physical performance and analyse its strengths and weaknesses. This is best done if the performance is a complex, self-paced closed skill, e.g. the triple jump in athletics. The strengths and weaknesses of each part of the performance, and how they affect the performance result, should be identified and noted. The weaknesses to be targeted for improvement should also be noted. In the **second part** of this task, an action plan must be produced to show progressive practices to remedy the weaknesses (chapter 4). These improvements should be noted (chapter 5) and an objective evaluation of this action plan made. Was it effective? If yes, how? If not, why not? How can it be improved on?
CCEA	**CCEA** requires you (for **Component 2** of Section 6) to produce evidence that you understand those aspects of the course that contribute to a healthy lifestyle. This is most effectively done in written form. As you have the length of the course to produce this evidence, it might be best to complete each aspect as it is covered during the course. You must show that you understand what a **balanced healthy lifestyle** consists of. Knowledge of levels of fitness (chapter 2) and how to assess them (chapter 5), diet (chapter 6), leisure and levels of exercise must also be shown (chapter 8). It is essential that you know the dangers associated with an unhealthy lifestyle (chapter 7). You must then **audit your own lifestyle** (possibly based on a diary) and produce a critical analysis of it. Then decide upon **changes** that will improve on this lifestyle and monitor the effectiveness of these implemented changes (good record-keeping is essential). You must also provide evidence of how these changes have brought about improvement (before and after assessments could be used). Do not forget that life goes on **outside school** and that this should be reflected in your submission.

1 The major body systems

The following topics are covered in this chapter:

- The skeletal system
- The muscular system
- The circulatory system
- The respiratory system

1.1 The skeletal system

LEARNING SUMMARY

After studying this section you should be able to:

- describe the functions of the skeleton
- describe the main bones of the body
- describe the main types of joints
- understand the importance of types of cartilage

N.B. See chapter 4 for Nervous System; see chapter 6 for Digestive System.

Functions of the skeleton

AQA	✓
EDEXCEL	✓
OCR	✓
WJEC	✓
CCEA	✓

> Make sure you are able to describe each function.

There are 206 bones in the skeleton, which have four main functions:

- **Blood production:** this takes place within the cavities of the long bones.
- **Protection:** soft tissue and delicate organs of the body, such as the brain, the heart and the lungs, are surrounded by protective bones.
- **Support:** without the skeleton we would not be able to keep our shape. Also, some organs are suspended from bony tissue.
- **Movement:** if muscles could not pull on several rigid bones it would not be possible for us to move.

The skeleton is made up of a large number of bones joined together (see Figure 1.1). 29 vertebrae make up the vertebral column (back bone). They are all separate bones, except for those that make up the coccyx, which are fused together. The joints between each pair of vertebrae individually provide little movement, but together provide a wide range of movement. Small discs of cartilage between each pair of movable vertebrae allow the bones to move without friction. The top two vertebrae are called the atlas and axis and they allow the head to move in all directions (see Figure 1.3). The column's main functions are to support weight, allow movement and protect the spinal cord (see Chapter 4).

The skeleton is sub-divided into two main parts:

- **Axial** – the **axial** skeleton, around which other bones move, includes the **skull** and the **thoracic vertebrae**.
- **Appendicular** – the **appendicular** skeleton includes the bones attached directly or indirectly to the axial skeleton. These include the **shoulder** and **hip girdles**, and the **arms** and **legs**.

Figure 1.1 The human skeleton

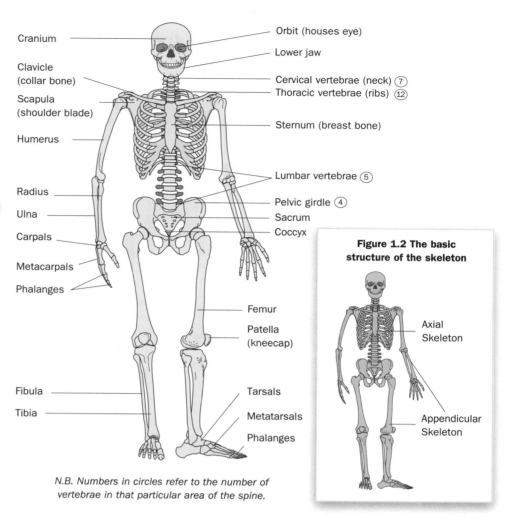

Cranium

Clavicle (collar bone)

Scapula (shoulder blade)

Humerus

Learn the names, shapes and positions of the major bones in the body.

Radius

Ulna

Carpals

Metacarpals

Phalanges

Orbit (houses eye)

Lower jaw

Cervical vertebrae (neck) ⑦
Thoracic vertebrae (ribs) ⑫

Sternum (breast bone)

Lumbar vertebrae ⑤

Pelvic girdle ④

Sacrum

Coccyx

Femur

Patella (kneecap)

Fibula

Tibia

Tarsals

Metatarsals

Phalanges

N.B. Numbers in circles refer to the number of vertebrae in that particular area of the spine.

Figure 1.2 The basic structure of the skeleton

Axial Skeleton

Appendicular Skeleton

KEY POINT

The places where two or more bones meet are called joints.

Joints and cartilage

The major types of joint are listed in the table below. Joint types (i) to (vi) are all synovial joints (see page 13). Joint type (vii) is the odd one out – this type of joint has no movement.

Table 1.1 Types of joints

Type	How Strong	Position in the Body	Range of Movement
(i) Ball and socket	Very strong	Hip/shoulder	Full
(ii) Hinge	Fairly strong	Elbow	Limited
(iii) Saddle	Fairly weak	Base of thumb	Limited
(iv) Condyloid	Weak	Wrist	Two ways only
(v) Pivot	Fairly strong	Neck	Rotation only
(vi) Slightly movable	Weak	Vertebrae (spine)	Depends on position
(vii) Immovable		Skull Sacrum	None None

The range of movement at the joints is shown in Figure 1.3. This in turn allows for the movements of the body limbs, as shown in Figure 1.4.

Figure 1.3 Range of movement at joints

(i) Ball and socket joint
The ball-shaped end of the femur fits into a cup-shaped socket in the pelvis and allows for movement in all directions.

Pelvis

Femur

Hip

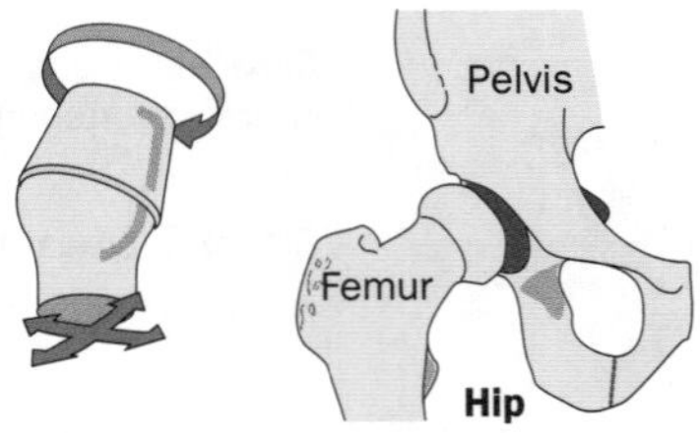

(ii) Hinge joint
Movement is allowed in one plane only.

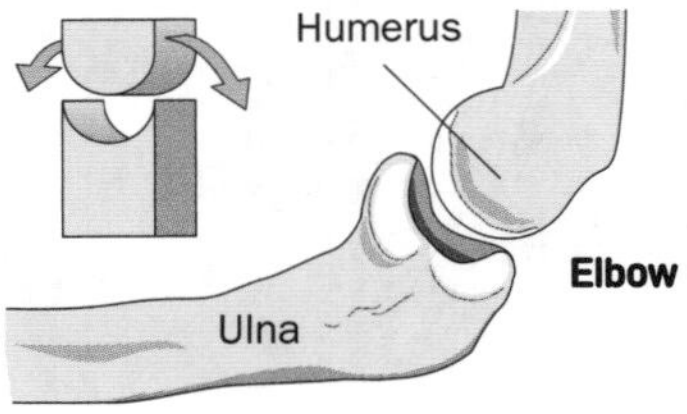

Humerus

Elbow

Ulna

(iii) Saddle joint
The opposing convex and concave surfaces of the two bones allow movement in two directions.

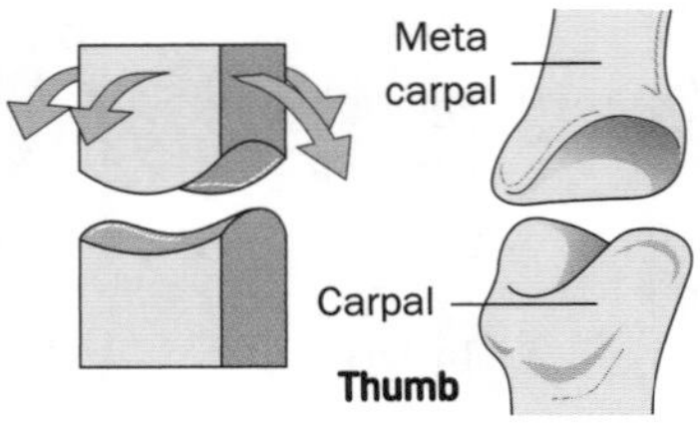

Meta carpal

Carpal

Thumb

(iv) Condyloid joint
The full convex shape of one bone end fits into the full concave shape of an adjoining bone. This allows for movement in all directions, but ligaments prevent rotation.

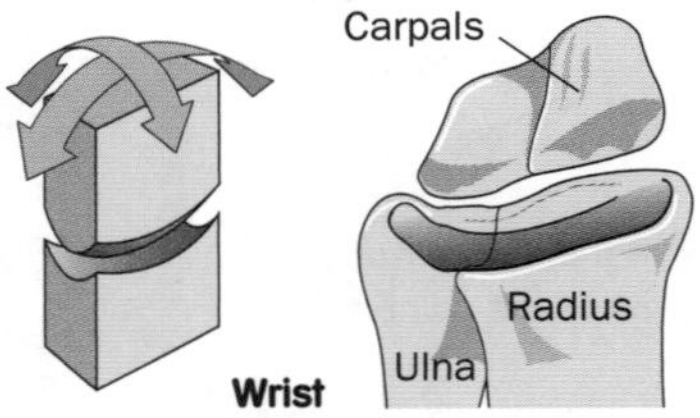

Carpals

Radius

Ulna

Wrist

(v) Pivot joint
In the case of the atlas and axis vertebrae, a circular section of the atlas sits on top of the peg shape of the axis. In the case of the radius and ulna, the radius is held within a fibrous ring attached to the ulna. Both these joints allow rotation to take place.

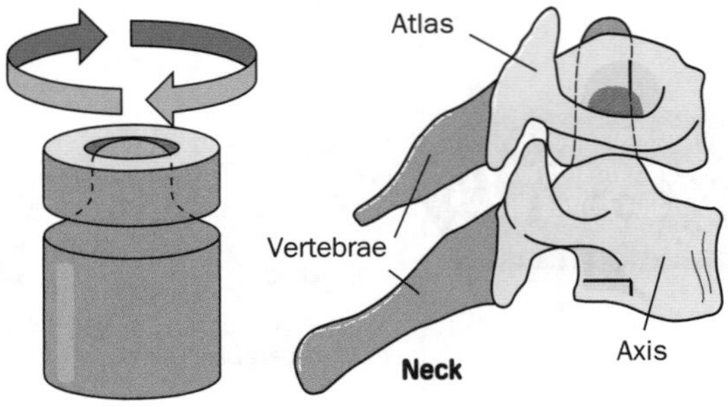

Atlas

Vertebrae

Axis

Neck

(vi) Slightly movable joint
When the back bends, the joint between two vertebrae moves only a small amount. The disc between the vertebrae is compressed on one side.

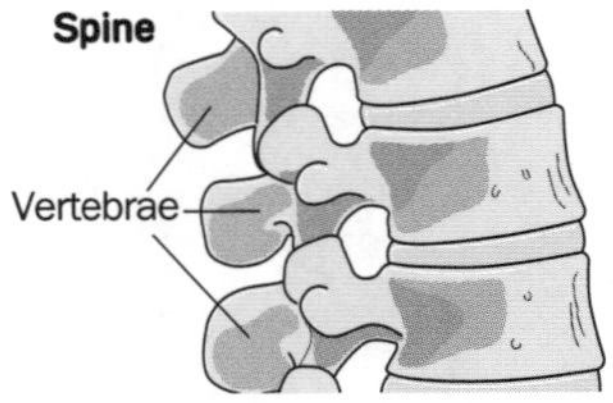

Spine

Vertebrae

(vii) Immovable joint
The bones have fused together.

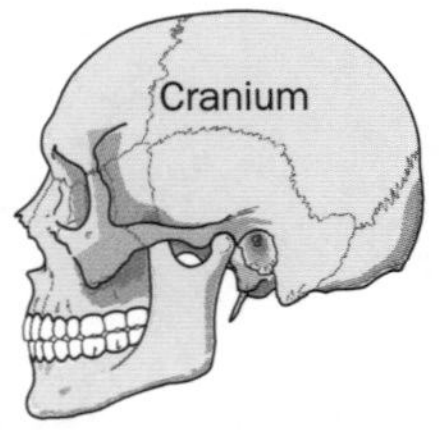

Cranium

Figure 1.4 Types of movement

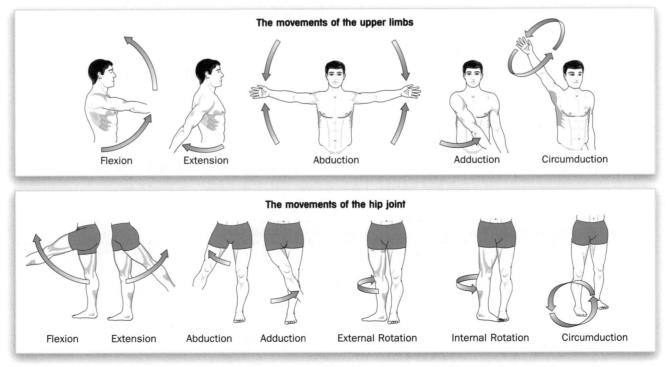

The movements of the upper limbs

Flexion   Extension   Abduction   Adduction   Circumduction

The movements of the hip joint

Flexion   Extension   Abduction   Adduction   External Rotation   Internal Rotation   Circumduction

> **Do not confuse ligaments and tendons. Ligaments attach bone to bone; tendons attach muscle to bone.**

Limb movement away from the centre of the body is abduction; limb movement towards the centre of the body is adduction; circular movement or circumduction combines all the movements of the hip or shoulder.

KEY POINT

Bones at movable joints are attached to each other by ligaments.

Movable joints are often referred to as synovial joints. This is because they are surrounded by a synovial membrane that contains synovial fluid. This fluid acts like the oil in a car engine: it lubricates the joint and helps to maintain a trouble-free movement. The knee joint is a good example of a synovial joint (see Figure 1.5).

The knee joint also shows the two main types of cartilage found at a joint:
- Articular
- Menisci

Articular cartilage is found at the end of the long bones. It is extremely hard, yet smooth and slippery. It protects the end of the bone from wear. Menisci (singular meniscus) look like crescent-shaped moons and, although they are attached to the long bones, they come between them. Menisci are made of a softer material and act as shock absorbers between the two long bones (see Figure 1.6).

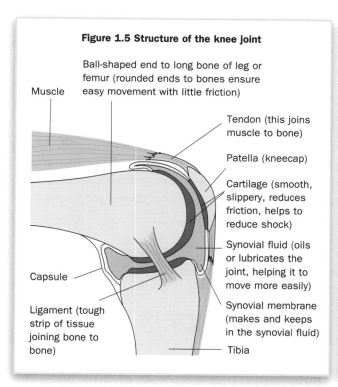

Figure 1.5 Structure of the knee joint

Muscle

Ball-shaped end to long bone of leg or femur (rounded ends to bones ensure easy movement with little friction)

Tendon (this joins muscle to bone)

Patella (kneecap)

Cartilage (smooth, slippery, reduces friction, helps to reduce shock)

Synovial fluid (oils or lubricates the joint, helping it to move more easily)

Capsule

Synovial membrane (makes and keeps in the synovial fluid)

Ligament (tough strip of tissue joining bone to bone)

Tibia

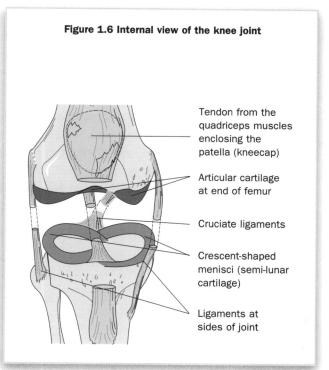

Figure 1.6 Internal view of the knee joint

Tendon from the quadriceps muscles enclosing the patella (kneecap)

Articular cartilage at end of femur

Cruciate ligaments

Crescent-shaped menisci (semi-lunar cartilage)

Ligaments at sides of joint

PROGRESS CHECK

1. List the four major functions of the skeleton.
2. What is the difference between a ligament and a tendon?
3. Explain the terms abduction and adduction.

3. Abduction is movement away from the centre of the body; adduction is movement towards the centre of the body.
2. Ligaments attach bone to bone; tendons attach muscle to bone.
1. Blood production, protection, support and movement.

1.2 The muscular system

LEARNING SUMMARY	After studying this section you should be able to:
	• describe the three major types of muscle fibre
	• describe how the muscles work together

Muscle fibre

AQA	✓
EDEXCEL	✓
OCR	✓
WJEC	✓
CCEA	✓

The body has three main types of muscle fibre:

- cardiac muscle fibre
- smooth muscle fibre
- skeletal muscle fibre.

Cardiac muscle fibre is found only in the heart. It contracts and relaxes continuously and its job is to ensure that blood is pumped around the body. The individual fibres of cardiac muscle are intertwined so that they can pull on each other (see Figure 1.7).

Smooth muscle fibre is often called **involuntary** muscle fibre as we have no control over its actions. Smooth muscle fibres make up the walls of certain soft tissues, such as the stomach, bladder and intestines. They allow the walls of these organs to stretch as they become full, and then return to their original size as they empty themselves. The fibres are laid side by side in layers to make up sheaths of smooth muscle (see Figure 1.8).

Skeletal muscle fibre is found in the muscles that we use to create movement. These muscles are also called **voluntary** muscles and **striated or striped** muscles: voluntary because we have control over them so that we can tell them when to contract or relax; striated or striped because under a microscope they have a striped appearance. These skeletal muscles make up the geography or shape of the body (see Figure 1.9).

Figure 1.7 Cardiac muscle fibre

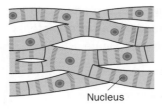

Nucleus

Figure 1.8 Smooth muscle fibre

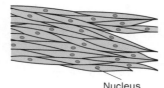

Nucleus

You should be able to name and place the major skeletal muscle groups of the body.

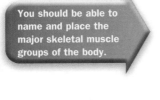

Do not use abbreviations.

Figure 1.9 The muscular system

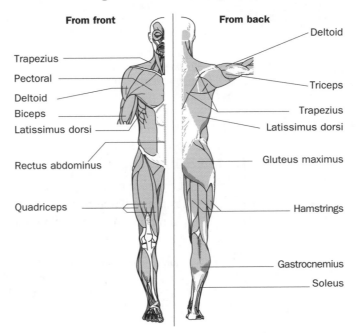

From front   From back

Deltoid

Trapezius

Pectoral

Deltoid

Biceps

Latissimus dorsi

Triceps

Trapezius

Latissimus dorsi

Rectus abdominus

Gluteus maximus

Quadriceps

Hamstrings

Gastrocnemius

Soleus

Each muscle contains a number of bundles of fibres, where the fibres all lie alongside each other. Each fibre is made up of many, much smaller **myofibrils**, which are made up of strands of protein called **actin** and **myosin**. The action of these two proteins sliding together brings about movement in the whole muscle (see Figure 1.10).

Figure 1.10 Skeletal muscle fibre

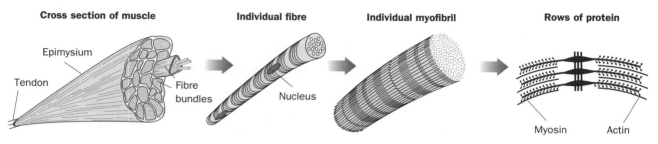

How muscles work

AQA	✓
EDEXCEL	✓
OCR	✓
WJEC	✓
CCEA	✓

Skeletal muscles are attached to the bones of the skeleton by a piece of connective tissue called a **tendon**. When muscles **contract**, they pull on bones at a joint and sometimes cause movement. These muscles never work alone; they always work in pairs or groups. As one muscle contracts, another will relax. We often describe these particular skeletal muscles by the work that they are doing. For example, a muscle that contracts and causes movement is called an **agonist** or **prime mover**; the muscle that relaxes is called an **antagonist**. Muscles that help the action of the prime mover are called **synergists**. They help to **stabilise** the joint and prevent undesirable movement.

Types of contraction

Isometric contractions are when the muscle fibres contract, yet stay the same length and the bones do not move. This type of contraction takes place, for example, in a rugby scrum or when the hands are pushed together.

Isotonic contractions are when the muscle fibres shorten and the bones move.

Eccentric contractions are when the muscle fibres lengthen under tension and the joint straightens. This movement takes place in an arm curl as the elbow is straightened when lowering the weight.

> It is important to be able to explain all of these terms. Any of them could come up in an exam.

In the case of the elbow, when the biceps contracts (isotonic contraction), the elbow joint closes. This is called **flexion**. At the same time, the triceps relaxes. In this action the biceps is the agonist and the triceps is the antagonist. However, when the triceps contracts the elbow joint will open. This is called **extension**. At the same time, the biceps will relax. In this action, the triceps is the agonist and the biceps is the antagonist (see Figure 1.11).

Figure 1.11 How muscles work together

Head of humerus
Scapula (shoulder blade)
Biceps muscle
Origin of triceps muscle
Triceps muscle
Flexion
Tendon
Radius
Ulna
Insertion of triceps muscle
Extension

The points where muscles are attached to the bones by tendons are called the points of **origin** and **insertion**. The point of origin is the point of attachment that does not move as flexion or extension takes place. The point of insertion is the point of attachment that does move during flexion or extension (see Figure 1.11).

Because of the job they do, skeletal muscle fibres are divided into two further muscle groups: **fast twitch** fibres and **slow twitch** fibres. We are all born with the same number of skeletal muscle fibres, but we all have a different number of fast or slow twitch fibres. The importance of this is illustrated in the table below.

Table 1.2 Fast twitch fibres and slow twitch fibres

Fast twitch	Shorter, thicker, contract quickly and exhaust quickly
Slow twitch	Longer, thinner, contract slowly and exhaust slowly

This means that...
- fast twitch fibres are suitable for explosive events, such as the shot put or the 100m race
- slow twitch fibres are more suited to endurance events, such as the marathon.

KEY POINT

Endurance training can make some fast twitch muscle fibres take on characteristics of slow twitch muscle fibres.

PROGRESS CHECK

1. Explain why smooth muscle fibre is often called involuntary fibre.
2. Where in the body will you find your...
   (a) deltoids? **(b)** gastrocnemius? **(c)** gluteous maximus?
3. What is the difference between an agonist and an antagonist muscle?

3. An agonist muscle contracts; an antagonist muscle relaxes as a joint moves.
2. **(a)** Point of shoulder. **(b)** Back of lower calf. **(c)** Buttocks.
1. We do not have control over the actions of these muscle fibres – they work automatically.

1.3 The circulatory system

LEARNING SUMMARY

After studying this section you should be able to:
- identify and describe the main parts of the circulatory system
- describe the pathway that blood follows
- describe the make-up and function of blood
- describe the effects of exercise on the circulatory system

Parts of the circulatory system

AQA	✓
EDEXCEL	✓
OCR	✓
WJEC	✓
CCEA	✓

The circulatory system has three main parts:
- the **heart**, which pushes blood around the body
- the **blood vessels**, which carry the blood around the body
- the **blood**, which acts as the transport system of the body.

The heart is made up of four distinct chambers and can, therefore, be described as two muscular pumps working side by side. Each upper chamber is called an **atrium** (*plural* atria) and each lower chamber is called a **ventricle**. The blood enters the heart through an atrium and leaves via a ventricle (see Figure 1.12). Blood enters the right atrium from the body, passes into the right ventricle and is then sent to the lungs. The left atrium receives blood from the lungs and passes it to the left ventricle, from where it passes round the body.

Figure 1.12 Structure of the heart showing direction of blood flow

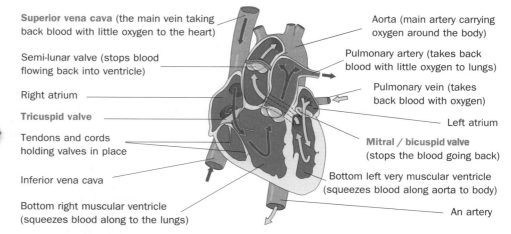

Superior vena cava (the main vein taking back blood with little oxygen to the heart)

Semi-lunar valve (stops blood flowing back into ventricle)

Right atrium

Tricuspid valve

Tendons and cords holding valves in place

Inferior vena cava

Bottom right muscular ventricle (squeezes blood along to the lungs)

Aorta (main artery carrying oxygen around the body)

Pulmonary artery (takes back blood with little oxygen to lungs)

Pulmonary vein (takes back blood with oxygen)

Left atrium

Mitral / bicuspid valve (stops the blood going back)

Bottom left very muscular ventricle (squeezes blood along aorta to body)

An artery

> You need to be able to draw a representation of the heart.

KEY POINT

The continuous contraction and relaxation of the heart means that blood does not flow evenly into the arteries. It is forced out of the heart in surges, which are called the pulse beat of the heart.

Blood pathway

> Always describe the pathway as though you are lying on your back looking up from the page.

When blood leaves the heart it travels either to the lungs or around the body. The blood on the right-hand side (looking out from the page) does not contain oxygen – it is **deoxygenated blood**. The blood on the left-hand side contains oxygen – it is **oxygenated blood**. (See Figure 1.13.)

KEY POINT

The path from the heart to the lungs and back is called the **pulmonary circuit**. The path from the heart to the body is called the **systemic circuit** (see Figure 1.14).

> Make sure you are able to draw and describe both the pulmonary and systemic circuits.

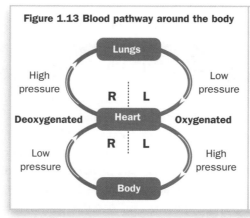

Figure 1.13 Blood pathway around the body

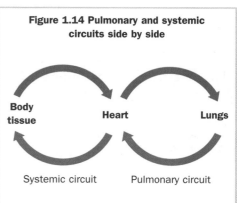

Figure 1.14 Pulmonary and systemic circuits side by side

The blood is forced around the body by the heart through different types of blood vessels:

- Vessels taking blood away from the heart are called **arteries**. They have thick elastic walls to absorb the pressure from the heart beat.
- Vessels bringing blood back to the heart are called **veins**. They have thinner, less elastic walls, but contain special valves to stop blood flowing backwards.
- Very small **capillaries** link arteries and veins. Capillaries are only one cell wide and have walls only one cell thick. This allows oxygen, food, carbon dioxide and waste products to pass between the muscles and the blood (see Figures 1.15 and 1.16).

Figure 1.15 The circulation of blood (as looking at the front of a person)

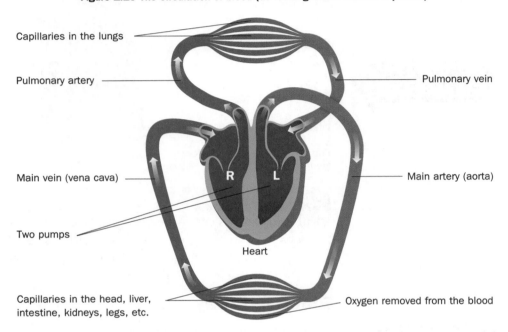

Capillaries in the lungs

Pulmonary artery

Pulmonary vein

Main vein (vena cava)

Main artery (aorta)

R   L

Two pumps

Heart

Capillaries in the head, liver, intestine, kidneys, legs, etc.

Oxygen removed from the blood

Figure 1.16 Exchange of substances at capillaries

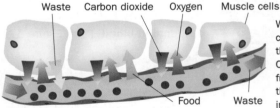

Waste   Carbon dioxide   Oxygen   Muscle cells

Food (e.g. glucose) from the digestive system or the liver is carried in the plasma. Oxygen from the lungs is carried by the red blood cells.

Waste from the cells is carried in the plasma. Carbon dioxide from respiration in the cells is carried in the plasma.

Food   Waste

A capillary vessel

Blood leaves the arteries in **pressure waves** called **pulse beats**. Where an artery is close to the body surface, the pulse rate can be measured – usually at the **radial artery** in the wrist and the **carotid** in the neck.

Blood pressure

AQA	✓
EDEXCEL	✓
OCR	✓
WJEC	✓
CCEA	✓

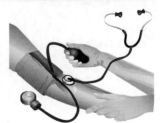

The pressure at which the blood leaves the heart is measured using either a stethoscope and **sphygmomanometer** or a modern **battery powered meter**. Two measurements are taken: **systolic pressure**, when the ventricles contract; and **diastolic pressure**, when the ventricles relax. A typical reading might be 120/80 for a normal person at rest. This level will rise during exercise.

Blood make-up and function

AQA ✓
EDEXCEL ✓
OCR ✓
WJEC ✓
CCEA ✓

Whole blood

Whole blood is made up of plasma, red blood cells, white blood cells and platelets. The table describes each of these parts.

> Remember that the cells are transported around the body in the plasma.

Table 1.3 Parts of blood

Plasma	Mainly water; acts as a transportation system; contains fibrinogen, a protein that is converted to fibrin during clotting.
Red blood cells	Bi-concave discs containing an oxygen-carrying substance called haemoglobin, which is reddish in colour.
White blood cells	There are two main types: phagocytes and lymphocytes. They are all irregular in shape. They help to fight toxins and bacteria.
Platelets	Tiny cells, without a nucleus, containing an enzyme that reacts when exposed to air, and aids clotting.

Function of blood

> **KEY POINT**
>
> The main functions of blood are transportation and protection.

Blood transports oxygen, carbon dioxide, nutrients, heat and waste products.

Table 1.4 Materials transported by blood

Oxygen	Transported from the lungs to all body tissue. The oxygen combines with the haemoglobin in the red blood cells where the capillaries meet the lungs. The haemoglobin gives up the oxygen to body tissue, e.g. the muscles, when required.
Carbon dioxide	Transported from all tissues to the lungs. The carbon dioxide forms a solution with the plasma which, when it reaches the lungs, gives up the carbon dioxide so that it can be exhaled.
Nutrients	Transported from the small intestine to all parts of the body. They are carried in solution within the plasma.
Heat	Transported from the muscles to all parts of the body. When the muscles work they get hot. As the blood moves around the body it transports this heat to the cooler parts so that an even temperature can be maintained. If the body becomes very hot the blood fills capillaries near the surface of the skin so that heat can escape from the body.
Waste products	Transported from all body tissues to the kidneys. Any waste product formed within the body is filtered through the kidneys so that it can be excreted.

> You should be able to describe the transportation function of blood.

Protection of the body by blood

Blood helps the body to protect itself in a number of ways. Table 1.5 describes them.

Table 1.5 Body protection by blood

Antitoxins	Produced by the lymphocytes to fight toxins (poisons) that might enter the body.
Antibodies	Produced by the lymphocytes to fight disease, and kept in the blood stream. They give immunity to certain illnesses.
Destruction	When bacteria cause a threat to the body, phagocytes attach themselves to, and 'eat', the harmful organisms.
Clotting	When a blood vessel is cut, the platelets combine forming a temporary plug to stop immediate blood loss. The enzymes in the platelets react with the air and cause the fibrinogen from the plasma to change into thread-like fibres of fibrin. These form a mesh, which seals the wound and prevents the entry of harmful bacteria. This mesh of fibres forms a scab.
Repair	The blood acts as a transport system for nutrients and other materials that are needed to repair damaged tissue, e.g. a cut on the body surface or broken capillaries that have formed a bruise under the surface of the skin.

You must be able to describe the protective functions of the blood.

Effects of exercise

The effects of exercise on the circulatory system depend on the type of physical activity performed, the intensity of the activity and the length of time spent on the activity.

Table 1.6 Main changes brought about during short-term exercise

Heart	• Increase in pulse rate. • Increase in blood pressure.
Blood	• More is brought into use. • Diverted from the soft organs. • Transports heat from the muscles to the body surface.

Muscles get priority for blood during exercise.

Table 1.7 Main effects of long-term high-intensity activity

Heart	• Increases in size. • Resting rate becomes lower. • Stroke volume is increased (i.e. more blood is pumped with each stroke). • Returns to resting rate faster after activity. • Helps prevent onset of coronary artery disease.
Blood	• Number of red blood cells is increased, thereby improving potential to transport oxygen. • Supply to muscle fibres is improved because more capillaries are available for blood to flow through. • Return of deoxygenated blood to the heart is improved.

Make sure you are able to differentiate between the effects of short-term and long-term exercise on the heart and blood.

1.4 The respiratory system

LEARNING SUMMARY

After studying this section you should be able to:

- describe the respiratory system and the breathing mechanism
- describe the effects of exercise on the respiratory system
- explain how oxygen and carbon dioxide are diffused

The respiratory tract

AQA ✓
EDEXCEL ✓
OCR ✓
WJEC ✓
CCEA ✓

There are three main parts of the respiratory system:

- **the nasal passages**
- **the trachea (windpipe)**
- **the lungs.**

The lungs are found within the **thoracic cavity** (chest). They are protected all round by the ribs, and protected at the bottom by a strong elastic sheath called the **diaphragm** (see Figure 1.17).

Figure 1.17   The main parts of the respiratory system

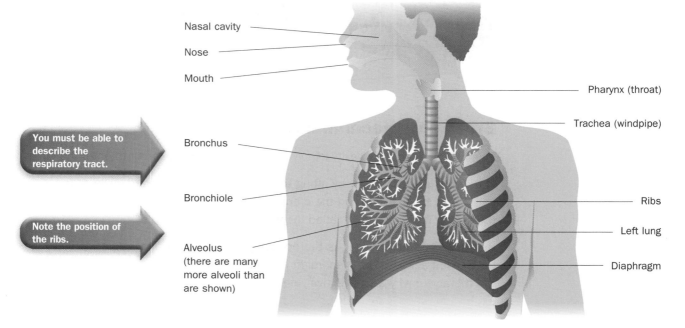

Nasal cavity

Nose

Mouth

Pharynx (throat)

Trachea (windpipe)

Bronchus

Bronchiole

Ribs

Left lung

Alveolus
(there are many
more alveoli than
are shown)

Diaphragm

> You must be able to describe the respiratory tract.

> Note the position of the ribs.

Air enters the body through the respiratory tract. It passes through the mouth and nose, and down the **trachea**, which divides into two **bronchi** – one into each lung. The bronchi sub-divide into **bronchioles** and end in **alveoli** (see Table 1.8).

Table 1.8 Respiratory tract

Air intake

Nasal passages: the nose and mouth.

Nasal cavity: the back of the nose above the mouth.

Trachea: a rigid tube, often called the windpipe.

Bronchus: each of the two bronchi leads into a lung.

Bronchioles: each bronchus subdivides again and again into smaller and smaller tubes called bronchioles.

Alveolus: the smallest of the bronchioles end in a cluster of air sacs called alveoli. Each alveolus is covered by a network of capillaries. It is here that gas exchange takes place.

Figure 1.18 The capillary network around the alveoli

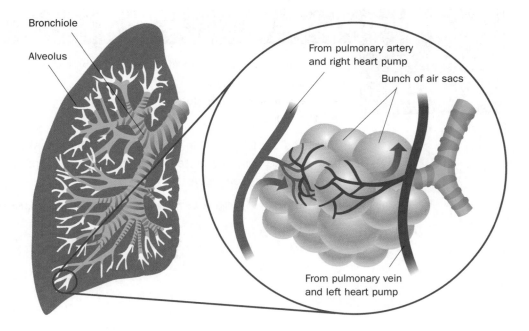

Bronchiole

Alveolus

From pulmonary artery and right heart pump

Bunch of air sacs

From pulmonary vein and left heart pump

Breathing mechanism

By making the thoracic cavity larger we create more space for air to enter the lungs.

The cavity is made larger by lifting the ribs forward and upward while at the same time pulling down on the diaphragm. This action effectively sucks air into the lungs. The process is called inspiration (see Figure 1.19).

Breathing out, or exhaling, is the opposite of inspiration. The ribs are pulled down and back and the diaphragm is pulled up. This action reduces the size of the thoracic cavity and effectively squeezes the air out. This process is called expiration (see Figure 1.20).

Figure 1.19 Inspiration – sucking air into the lungs

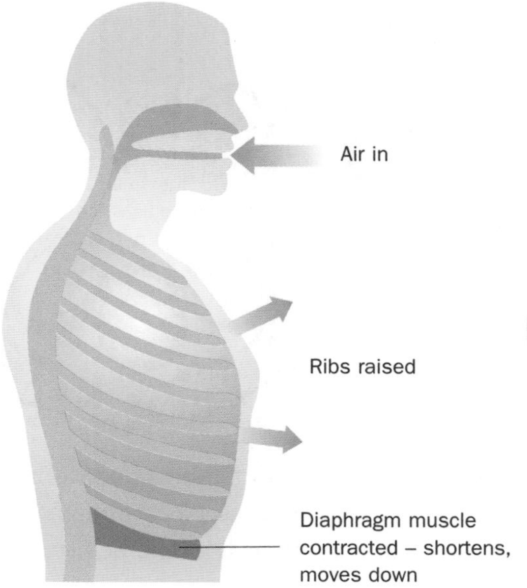

Air in

Ribs raised

Diaphragm muscle contracted – shortens, moves down

Figure 1.20 Expiration – squeezing air out of the lungs

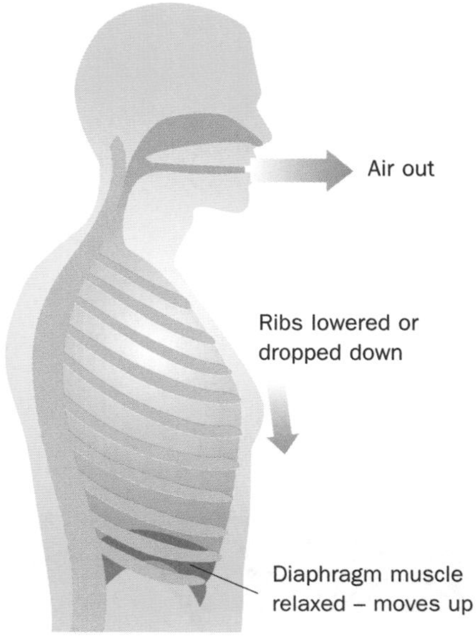

Air out

Ribs lowered or dropped down

Diaphragm muscle relaxed – moves up

Lung capacities

We measure the amount of air that can be inspired using a machine called a **spirometer**. This machine draws a line on a moving sheet of paper to show the amount of air inspired and expired over a given period. This total lung capacity is divided into sections (see Figure 1.21).

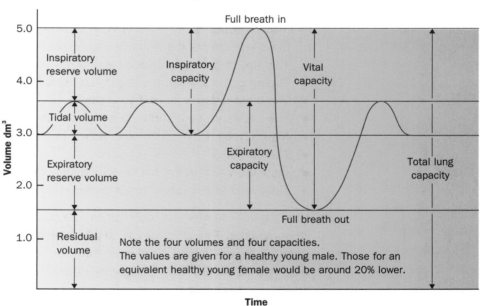

Figure 1.21 Spirometer trace

Full breath in

Inspiratory reserve volume

Inspiratory capacity

Vital capacity

Tidal volume

Volume dm³

Expiratory reserve volume

Expiratory capacity

Total lung capacity

Full breath out

Residual volume

Note the four volumes and four capacities.
The values are given for a healthy young male. Those for an equivalent healthy young female would be around 20% lower.

Time

After full expiration there is always a little air left in the lungs. This is called the residual volume.

Response to exercise

Exercise has a major effect on the lung capacity of an athlete. In the short term, breathing becomes more rapid and deeper during exercise. This means that more air is inspired during exercise and, therefore, more oxygen can be transferred to the blood stream. This is necessary to ensure that the muscles can work. This transfer of oxygen to the blood is called **gaseous exchange** (see Figure 1.22).

Figure 1.22 Detailed section of one air sac (alveolus) showing gaseous exchange

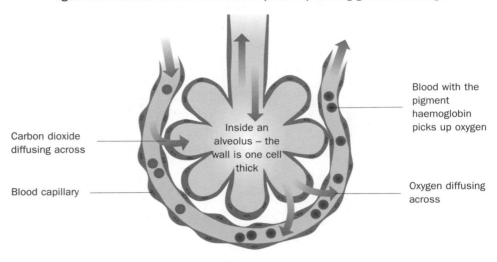

Blood with the pigment haemoglobin picks up oxygen

Carbon dioxide diffusing across

Inside an alveolus – the wall is one cell thick

Blood capillary

Oxygen diffusing across

> Do not confuse oxygen uptake with oxygen intake.

Not all oxygen is removed from the air when we breathe in at any one time. The amount of oxygen passed into the blood stream is called **oxygen uptake** and it depends on the type and intensity of the activity we are doing (see Table 1.9).

Table 1.9 Amount of O_2 and CO_2 present in inspired and expired air

	Inspired Air	Expired at Rest	Expired During Exercise
O_2	21%	17%	15%
CO_2	0.03%	3%	6%

Effects of exercise on the respiratory system

Although breathing becomes more rapid during exercise, the speed with which this occurs depends upon the amount of physical activity the individual is used to. The major effects that training has on the respiratory system are as follows:

- The size of the chest increases.
- The amount by which the chest can expand increases.
- The breathing rate at rest gets slower.
- The capillary web around the alveolus is increased.
- More alveoli are ready to pass gases to and from the blood.
- The exchange of gas is improved.
- Inspiratory and expiratory reserve volumes increase.
- Tidal volume increases during exercise.

After physical activity has taken place, the person will continue to breathe deeply for some time. This is to remove any **oxygen debt** that may have developed (see page 39). A well-trained, fit person, however, will revert to normal breathing faster than an untrained, unfit person. This is due to their more efficient breathing mechanisms.

PROGRESS CHECK

1. Identify the major organs of the respiratory system.
2. What is vital capacity?
3. Explain the term 'oxygen uptake'.

3. The amount of oxygen absorbed into the blood during each breath.
2. The combined total of the tidal volume, inspiratory reserve volume and expiratory reserve volume.
1. Nasal passages, windpipe / trachea and lungs.

Sample GCSE questions

1 Give the anatomical name for each of the following bones:

(a) Skull   Cranium

(b) Shoulder blade   Scapula

(c) Toes   Phalanges

(d) Collar bone   Clavicle   **(4)**

> Make sure that you spell these terms correctly.

2 Adduction and extension are two types of movement possible at a ball and socket joint. Give **three** other movement possibilities.

Flexion, Rotation, Circumduction, Abduction   **(3)**

> Any three of these would be satisfactory.

3 State which main muscle contracts for each of the following actions:

(a) Straightening the elbow.

Triceps

(b) Pulling your leg back at the hip.

Gluteals / Gluteus maximus

(c) Flexing your trunk so that you can bend forward.

Abdominals / Hip flexors / Rectus abdominus   **(4)**

> You have a choice with two parts of this question: one of two possible answers would be satisfactory in part (b) and one of three possible answers would be satisfactory in part (c). Make sure you learn the spellings well!

4 When the elbow flexes, which main muscle is the...

(a) antagonist?   Triceps

(b) agonist?   Biceps   **(2)**

> Simple answers are all that are required.

5 Give a function for each of the following:

(a) Red blood cells   Carry oxygen

(b) White blood cells   Fight bacteria, infection, disease

(c) Platelets   Clotting   **(3)**

> Only one of these is needed.

6 **(a)** In which part of the lungs does gaseous exchange take place?

Alveoli (plu.) / Alveolus (sing.)

(b) Give the anatomical name for the windpipe.

Trachea

(c) What happens to the diaphragm and ribs during expiration?

The diaphragm goes up / goes dome-shaped. The ribs move down and in.   **(3)**

> You must state the full movement of the ribs to get the marks.

Exam practice questions

1 Give another name for the thigh bone.

.... **(1)**

2 Give **two** functions of the skeleton.

(a) ....

(b) .... **(2)**

3 Explain the following movements at a joint:

(a) Flexion ....

(b) Extension ....

(c) Circumduction .... **(3)**

4 Describe ligaments and their functions at synovial joints.

....

....

....

.... **(4)**

5 List the **three** types of muscle tissue found in the body and give an example of where each one can be found.

....

....

.... **(6)**

2 Fitness

The following topics are covered in this chapter:

- **Definitions of fitness**
- **Physical fitness**
- **Components of physical fitness**
- **Motor fitness**
- **Improving fitness**

2.1 Definitions of fitness

LEARNING SUMMARY

After studying this section you should be able to:

- explain what fitness is
- recall the major definitions of fitness

What is fitness?

AQA	✓
EDEXCEL	✓
OCR	✓
WJEC	✓
CCEA	✓

Fitness can mean different things to different people. For example, a weight-lifting champion has a different concept of fitness from that of a marathon runner.

There are several definitions of fitness:

- The ability to perform physical tasks efficiently and effectively. (CCEA)
- The ability to meet the daily physical demands of work and play without excessive fatigue and still have something in reserve. (AQA)
- The ability to meet the demands of the environment. (Edexcel)
- A physical condition, which is the result of differing fitness components working together to influence overall physical efficiency. (WJEC)

> Make sure you are able to quote the definition given by your exam board.

What is common to all these definitions is the idea that physical fitness is the ability to perform **physical activity efficiently** without placing **undue strain** on the body. When considering the idea of physical fitness we should always ask the question, 'Fit for what?'

In trying to answer this question we must take into account that fitness is divided into **two** main areas:

- **physical fitness**
- **motor fitness.**

PROGRESS CHECK

1. What two aspects are common to the major definitions of fitness described in this topic?
2. What two areas is fitness divided into?

1. Physical activity carried out efficiently, without undue stress.
2. Physical fitness and motor fitness.

2.2 Physical fitness

LEARNING SUMMARY

After studying this section you should be able to:

- explain physical fitness
- describe the effects that physical activity has on the body systems
- understand the terms 'aerobic fitness' and 'anaerobic fitness'

What is physical fitness?

AQA ✓
EDEXCEL ✓
OCR ✓
WJEC ✓
CCEA ✓

KEY POINT

Physical fitness can be described as 'the ability to meet the physical and physiological demands made by a particular sporting activity'.

How does physical activity affect us?

The effects of participation in physical activity will alter the way in which various body systems work (see Table 2.1).

Table 2.1 Changes observed in some of the body systems brought on by physical training

	At rest	During activity
Depth of breathing	8 litres/minute	25 litres/minute
Pulse rate	75 beats/minute	190+ beats/minute
Stroke volume	100 ml/beat	200 ml/beat
Cardiac output*	7 litres/minute	35+ litres/minute
O_2 used per min	250 ml/minute	4500+ ml/minute
Size of O_2 debt developed	none	10+ litres

Be aware of these significant changes.

* Cardiac output is the volume of blood pumped by the left ventricle of the heart in 1 minute. It is measured in litres per minute. The sign for cardiac output is Q.

The ability of the body to cope with these changes will depend upon how prepared it is for the demands that are being made upon it.

KEY POINT

The body adjusts to the demands that are regularly made upon it.

Someone who runs a little further each day will gradually find it easier to run for longer as their respiratory system becomes more efficient. When someone's body systems can meet the demands of exercise without undue stress, they are said to be in a **normal state**. However, the normal state will change as more and more regular physical demands are made. The body is able to adjust to regular participation in physical activity.

Aerobic and anaerobic fitness

All physical activities demand a combination of **aerobic** and **anaerobic** fitness.

Aerobic fitness, also known as cardio-respiratory endurance, is required for activities of low intensity, often over a long period of time. These activities meet their energy demands from oxygen (O_2).

Anaerobic fitness is required for activities of high intensity over a short period of time. These activities meet their energy demands from glucose. (See Chapter 3.)

PROGRESS CHECK

1. How can physical fitness be described?
2. What happens to the body when regular demands are made on it?
3. What does 'Q' stand for?

3. Cardiac output (the amount of blood pumped out by the left ventricle in 1 minute).
2. It adjusts to these demands.
1. The ability to meet the physical and physiological demands made by a particular sporting activity.

2.3 Components of physical fitness

LEARNING SUMMARY

After studying this section you should be able to:

- understand the five major components of physical fitness

The five main components of physical fitness

AQA	✓
EDEXCEL	✓
OCR	✓
WJEC	✓
CCEA	✓

Physical fitness can be said to have five major components: strength, stamina, speed, suppleness and somatotype. These are often referred to as the 5 Ss (see Figure 2.1).

Ensure that you can list the five Ss.

Figure 2.1 The five main components of physical fitness

* The full influence of somatotype, often referred to as 'body composition', is discussed in Chapter 6.
**Suppleness is often referred to as flexibility or mobility.

The balance of these components required by a sportsperson varies according to the demands of each particular sport.

Strength

KEY POINT

Strength is defined as the ability to use muscles to apply force to overcome resistance.

There are three types of strength, each being suited to a different physical activity: static strength, explosive strength, and dynamic strength (see Table 2.2).

You must know, and be able to differentiate between, these three types of strength.

Table 2.2 Analysis of strength types

	Static strength	Explosive strength	Dynamic strength
Activity example	Tug of war Rugby scrum	Shot put High jump	Rowing 100m sprint
Body state	Stays the same	Moves fast	Moves fast
Distance moved	Little or none	Little	Can be considerable
Time taken	Varies, but not long	Small amount	Can be considerable
Muscle state / Fibre changes	Fibres stay the same length	Fibre length changes quickly	Fibre length changes quickly and repeatedly

Figure 2.2 An example of static strength combined with balance

Speed

> **KEY POINT**
>
> Speed is defined as the shortest time taken to move the body, or a body part, over a specific distance.

The ability to move the body quickly is essential in many sporting activities. Speed may be assisted by many different body parts, for example, the legs in running, and the legs and arms in swimming.

In some sports only one part of the body is expected to move fast, for example, in fencing it is the rapid straightening of the arm that can win a point; in karate it might be the fast movement of the foot that wins a point. In other sports, such as archery, speed of the body or limbs makes little or no contribution towards the accuracy demanded in competition.

Stamina

> **KEY POINT**
>
> Stamina is defined as the ability to perform strenuous activity over a long period of time.

The term 'cardiovascular' relates to cardio (meaning 'heart') and vascular (meaning 'blood vessels').

Stamina is often referred to as **cardiovascular fitness** or **muscular endurance**. In order to meet the requirements of cardiovascular fitness, there must be a continuous ready supply of oxygen to the muscles so that energy can be produced and waste matter can be removed (see Chapter 3).

If the body is worked too hard over a long period of time, then an **oxygen debt** will develop (see page 39). This will eventually result in the build-up of **lactic acid** in the muscles, which in turn brings on a feeling of fatigue and possible cramp in some muscles.

Many sports demand stamina, for example, rowing and long-distance running.

Suppleness

KEY POINT

Suppleness is defined as the range of movement possible at a joint or joints.

Suppleness is often referred to as **flexibility** or **mobility**. Suppleness is affected by the type of joint and the muscle attachments to it. Some joints, such as the hip, move freely, giving a wide range of movement (see Figure 2.3).

Figure 2.3 This activity shows a wide range of movement at the hip

Other joints, such as those between the vertebrae, have a very limited range of movement. They overcome this deficiency by working together to give a more extensive range of movement.

Training can increase the suppleness of all types of joints. A greater range of movement at a joint may be an advantage in some sports. For example, the butterfly swimmer needs to have a wide range of movement in the shoulders, whilst the weight-lifter places greater emphasis on strength and requires only a limited range of movement at the shoulder.

Table 2.3 Physical fitness components of some sporting activities

You should be able to identify a sporting activity to illustrate each physical fitness component.

	Strength	**Stamina**	**Speed**	**Suppleness**
Rowing	Yes	Yes	Some	Some
Aerobics	Some	Yes	Yes	Yes
Skating	Some	Some	Some	Some
Soccer	Some	Yes	Some	Some
Archery	Some	Little	Little	Little

PROGRESS CHECK

1. Define the term 'physical fitness'.
2. What single change is brought on in all body systems by physical training?
3. What are the main types of strength? Give an example of each.

3. Static, e.g. tug of war; Explosive, e.g. shot put; Dynamic, e.g. rowing.
2. They all increase the amount of work they do.
1. The ability to meet the physical and physiological demands made by a particular sporting activity.

2.4 Motor fitness

LEARNING SUMMARY

After studying this section you should be able to:

- understand the term 'motor fitness'
- understand the main components of motor fitness

What is motor fitness?

AQA ✓
EDEXCEL ✓
OCR ✓
WJEC ✓
CCEA ✓

> **KEY POINT**
>
> Motor fitness can be defined as the ability to perform successfully in a given sporting context.

To achieve success in any sporting context, all components of physical fitness are needed. However, motor fitness will affect more directly the sportsperson's ability to perform the skills essential to the chosen physical activity.

The main components of motor fitness are:

- **Power** – strength and speed working together.
- **Agility** – the ability to change body position and direction quickly and with precision.
- **Coordination** – the ability to perform complex motor tasks involving several skills, in sequence, as in hurdling.
- **Balance** – an awareness of the body's position in a fast-changing physical situation, such as in gymnastic activity on the beam.
- **Reaction** – the time taken to respond to a given stimulus.
- **Attitude** – the psychological approach brought by the sportsperson to the sporting situation, often described as the 'will to win' factor. This element of motor fitness is often overlooked.

> These components are often referred to as the skill-related aspects of fitness.

> Make sure you can describe each of the main components of motor fitness.

Figure 2.4 Major components of motor fitness

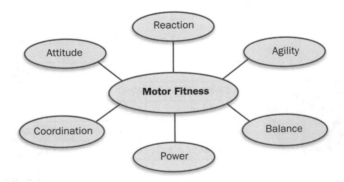

> **PROGRESS CHECK**
>
> 1. Define the term 'motor fitness'.
> 2. List four components of motor fitness.
> 3. Give another name for the components of motor fitness.

1. The ability to perform successfully in a sporting context.
2. **Any four from:** Power; Agility; Coordination; Balance; Reaction; Attitude.
3. Skill-related aspects.

2.5 Improving fitness

LEARNING SUMMARY

After studying this section you should be able to:

- understand the five guiding principles related to fitness improvement
- understand the **FITT** principles relating to fitness improvement

Fitness principles

AQA	✓
EDEXCEL	✓
OCR	✓
WJEC	✓
CCEA	✓

The physical fitness of the human body can always be improved. This can be done by following a relevant training programme. Some programmes are more effective than others. There are five guiding principles that can help you to decide on an effective programme. They are:

- Specificity
- Progression
- Overload
- Reversibility
- Tedium.

> The letters SPORT will help you to remember these principles.

Specificity

Training should be specific. This means that it should concentrate on the particular needs of the performer. Lifting weights, for example, will increase muscle strength but it will have little effect on aerobic capacity.

Not only should the training be specific to the particular sport, but it should also be specific to the parts of the body that contribute most to that sport. If upper body strength is required then exercise concentrating on the arms and chest will be needed. If both speed and endurance are required then exercises should be included with these requirements in mind.

> You should be able to name exercises specific to different body parts.

A programme may well be designed to be specific to a person returning from injury. If the muscles of one leg are recovering from a strain or pull they cannot be worked as hard as those of the other leg (that have not been damaged). Lower levels of stress should be put on recently repaired body tissue. By carefully designing a programme specific to the recovering body part, effective rehabilitation should be achieved.

Progression

A training session should always be within the capabilities of the individual. Although stress needs to be placed on the body systems in order for the training to be effective, too much stress too soon can cause injury.

> Remember that progression should be gradual.

If the overload of the body systems is increased at a steady, attainable rate, then improvements can be easily monitored and progression noted. However, it must be remembered that the body adapts and begins to find the harder programmes less demanding as time goes by. Therefore, the overload must be increased, otherwise progression will stop.

Overload

Overload is the term used to describe activities that impose greater demands than usual on the body.

The overload principle aims to put the body systems under stress, i.e. if excessive demand is put on a muscle repeatedly, then more fibres will be prepared for work; if excessive demand is put on the body's aerobic system, it will produce more red blood cells so that more oxygen can be taken up and used more effectively.

It is possible to increase **aerobic activity**, **muscular strength** and **flexibility** by using the overload principle. This improvement can be attained in three ways:

- By increasing the **intensity** of the activity – this might mean that we have to run faster, lift heavier weights or stretch further during training. This builds up over a period of time.
- By increasing the **frequency** of the activity – this means that there should be more training sessions with shorter rest periods between them.
- By increasing the **duration** of the activity – this means that the length of each training session should be increased progressively.

> **KEY POINT**
>
> If all three methods of overload were to be used at one time then training sessions would be harder work, more frequent and would take longer.

Reversibility

Just as the body adapts to greater stress, it will also adapt to less stress being put upon it. If training is to stop for any reason for a period of time, fitness will be impaired. It should be noted that the body adapts to lower stress levels far more quickly than it does to high stress levels.

Anaerobic activities are affected less than aerobic ones as they do not need vast amounts of oxygen. The aerobic capacity of muscles deteriorates very quickly. If the muscles are not used they begin to **atrophy**: this means that they will waste away and become smaller and thinner. Weaker muscles are more prone to injury. It is estimated that strength is lost three times more quickly than it is gained.

Tedium

Training can be boring. When boredom (tedium) sets in, the training becomes less effective. The onset of boredom can be avoided by using a variety of training methods or by shifting the emphasis of the training programme.

FITT principle

When referring to principles of training, many people like to use the mnemonic FITT. This is a slightly different way of remembering the principles just described.

These principles all relate to specificity, overload and progression, but be aware that reversibility and tedium are also essential components.

FITT stands for:
F – frequency (i.e. how often you should exercise)
I – intensity (i.e. how hard you should exercise)
T – time (i.e. how long you should exercise for)
T – type (i.e. what exercises you consider suitable for your chosen sport)

> **PROGRESS CHECK**
>
> 1. List the three ways in which overload can be attained.
> 2. Explain how duration can be used to increase overload.
>
> 2. The length of each training session should be increased.
> 1. Increase in intensity, frequency, duration.

Sample GCSE questions

1 Define the following terms:

(a) Cardiac output

The volume of blood pumped by the left ventricle in one minute.

(3)

> The emphasis is three-fold, namely: the volume of blood; the left ventricle; and one minute.

(b) Stamina

The ability to perform strenuous activity over a long period of time.

(2)

> The emphasis is strenuous activity and period of time.

(c) Power

A combination of speed and strength.

(2)

> 'Force multiplied by distance' would also be acceptable.

2 Give an example of each of the following:

(a) Agility in a team game

Side stepping, dodging in rugby.

(1)

> It helps to clarify your answer if you can relate it to a specific sport.

(b) Reaction time

A quick start in a swimming race or athletics sprint in response to a starting gun.

(1)

> This is a reaction to a stimulus, e.g. the starting gun.

(c) Balance

Holding a hand stand in gymnastics.

(1)

> Always mention an activity when describing terms such as these.

3 Name the **five** main components of physical fitness.

Suppleness, strength, stamina, speed and somatotype

(5)

> These are called the 5 Ss.

4 When considering the three types of strength, what does the term 'muscle state' refer to?

The changes of the muscle fibre lengths.

(2)

> Make sure you are able to link each change to the strength type.

Exam practice questions

1 Mary is an up-and-coming tennis player. She is advised that her standard of play will improve if she increases her level of fitness. She starts training three times a week, for an hour each session.

Week 1

Session 1   Running session

Session 2   Speed work on court holding a racket

Session 3   Weights session

(a) State which aspect of the FITT principle relates to each of the following:

(i) 'An hour each session' ....

(ii) 'Three times a week' ....

(iii) 'Speed work on court holding a racket' .... **(3)**

There are several other principles of training in addition to the FITT principle. The following questions relate to these other principles.

(b) Which principle of training needs to be applied to the programme to ensure that Mary's fitness continues to improve?

.... **(1)**

(c) Which principle of training should be applied to Mary's programme to reduce the chance of injury?

.... **(1)**

(d) Which principle of training will apply if Mary stops training for a couple of months?

.... **(1)**

(e) Which principle of training needs to be considered if Mary wants to improve her grip strength on the racket?

.... **(1)**

3 Training methods and programmes

The following topics are covered in this chapter:

- Training threshold
- Oxygen debt
- Training methods
- Exercise programmes
- Training requirements

3.1 Training threshold

LEARNING SUMMARY

After studying this section you should be able to understand:

- the value of a training threshold
- how to establish maximum heart rate
- how to work out a training threshold

What is a training threshold?

AQA	✓
EDEXCEL	✓
OCR	✓
WJEC	✓
CCEA	✓

Training can be effective only if the body systems are put under stress. There must be a suitable element of **overload** in any training programme. What needs to be established is the **safe, yet effective**, level at which training should take place. This is known as the **training threshold rate (TTR)**. Physical work done below this level will have little or no effect on the improvement of fitness. However, work done that is well above this level can lead to injury (see Figure 3.1).

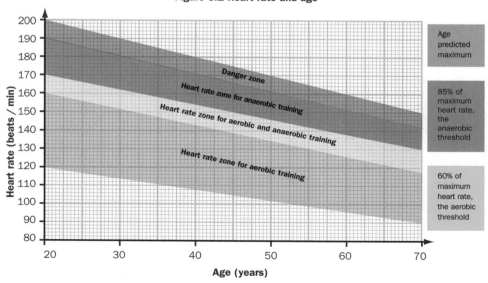

Figure 3.1 Heart rate and age

Danger zone

Heart rate zone for anaerobic training

Heart rate zone for aerobic and anaerobic training

Heart rate zone for aerobic training

Age predicted maximum

85% of maximum heart rate, the anaerobic threshold

60% of maximum heart rate, the aerobic threshold

Heart rate (beats / min) / Age (years)

KEY POINT

Training threshold rate is a safe and effective level to work at.

Maximum heart rate

Ensure that you are aware of the different methods of establishing maximum heart rate.

To be able to establish your correct training threshold, it is important to establish your **maximum heart rate** in beats per minute. Many people use the accepted formula that your maximum heart rate is always **220 beats per minute minus your age**. Some suggest **180** as the maximum, whilst others claim that it varies with age. These are all rather crude, but essentially safe, ways of establishing a maximum heart rate, as they take into account that the maximum declines as a person gets older. The validity of these methods has been shown through scientific research.

A more exact and scientific way of establishing maximum heart rate is to undertake a test (e.g. on a treadmill). This means a person has to work at **maximal** effort for a given period of time.

Using the maximum heart rate

However the maximum heart rate is established, it can be used to determine the appropriate **training threshold rate** for an individual. Below are four ways in which this can be done. Each is effective in its own way.

- **The 180 method** – deduct your age from 180. This assumes that your maximum heart rate is 180. Therefore, the safe and effective training threshold for a 40-year-old person would be 140 (180 – 40 = 140).

Remember that notional is not the same as maximal.

- **The 70% to 80% method** – this is based on a person working at 70% to 80% of a **notional** maximum heart rate that is related to a given age (see Table 3.1).

Table 3.1 Table used to calculate training thresholds

Age	Maximum heart rate (beats per minute)	Safe working rate (beats per minute)
20	200	140/160
30	190	133/152
40	180	126/144
50	170	119/136

You should be able to work out a threshold rate for a given set of figures.

The following two methods **presuppose** a maximum heart rate:

- **The 60% method** – this calculates the threshold level by adding 60% of the range of your heart rate to the resting pulse rate. For example: If a person's resting pulse rate is 80 and his maximum heart rate is 180, then the range is 100 (180 – 80 = 100). 60% of the range is 60 so the threshold rate is 140 (80 + 60 = 140).

Note that to use the 60% method and Karvonen's formula, a person must be able to establish his / her own maximum heart rate correctly.

- **Karvonen's formula** – this establishes the threshold as follows: Establish a person's resting pulse rate, for example, 60 and establish her maximum heart rate, for example, 200 then the range is 140 (200 – 60 = 140). 70% of the range is 98, so the threshold rate is 158 (98 + 60 = 158).

KEY POINT

The 60% method is more suitable for strength work, while Karvonen's formula is more suitable for aerobic training.

PROGRESS CHECK

1. Why should physical activity be carried out at the TTR?
2. Which two methods of establishing TTR presuppose a maximum heart rate?

1. It is a safe and effective level to perform at.
2. The 60% method and Karvonen's formula.

3.2 Oxygen debt

LEARNING SUMMARY

After studying this section you should be able to understand:

- how ATP supplies muscles with energy
- the terms 'aerobic' and 'anaerobic'

ATP

AQA	✓
EDEXCEL	✓
OCR	✓
WJEC	✓
CCEA	✓

You must be able to describe this process.

Training requires a great deal of muscular exertion. This means that throughout exercise the muscles are continually contracting and relaxing. This muscular exertion requires **energy**. Energy comes from a substance called **adenosine triphosphate (ATP)** which, during exercise, breaks down to a second substance called **adenosine diphosphate (ADP)**. It is this breakdown that produces the energy. The energy that is stored within **ATP** comes from the reaction between **glucose** and **oxygen** (see page 79).

KEY POINT

ATP is stored in muscle fibres, but is quickly used up.

Aerobic and anaerobic activity

Aerobic activity – If a lot of oxygen is present, then energy production is carried out **aerobically**. As this type of physical activity requires large amounts of oxygen, the level of work must be of low intensity, but it may continue for a long period of time. Long-distance running is an aerobic activity.

Aerobic = With oxygen
Anaerobic = Without oxygen

Anaerobic activity – If there is a shortage of oxygen, then energy production is carried out **anaerobically**. This type of physical work is usually of high intensity, lasts for a short period of time and requires a great deal of energy, but it does not have time to get lots of oxygen to the muscles. The 100-metre sprint is an anaerobic activity.

If anaerobic activity takes place for a long period of time the muscles soon become exhausted. This is due to a condition called oxygen debt.

Retained lactic acid can cause stiffness the next day.

Strenuous exercise uses up all ATP stores and causes a build-up of **lactic acid**. This is a **toxic** (poisonous) substance that causes the muscles to stop working. Lactic acid can only be removed in the presence of oxygen. Upon completion of hard strenuous exercise it is essential that the oxygen debt is repaid. Large amounts of oxygen are needed for this **oxygen recovery**. This is why we pant after hard exercise. In this way, ATP stores are replenished and lactic acid is removed from the muscular system (see Figure 3.2).

Figure 3.2 Lactic acid energy system

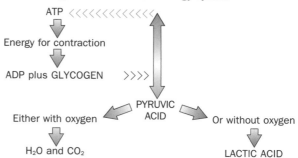

ATP ‹‹‹‹‹‹‹‹‹‹‹‹‹
Energy for contraction
ADP plus GLYCOGEN ››››
PYRUVIC ACID
Either with oxygen
Or without oxygen
H_2O and CO_2
LACTIC ACID

By establishing a suitable training threshold rate it should be possible to train effectively, whilst at the same time avoiding the build-up of lactic acid, which could bring training to a premature end.

> **PROGRESS CHECK**
>
> 1. Which substance do we get energy from?
> 2. What is the major difference between aerobic and anaerobic activity?
> 3. What builds up in the muscles during prolonged anaerobic activity?
>
> 1. ATP (adenosine triphosphate). 2. Aerobic activity uses oxygen at the time of exercise; anaerobic activity does not use oxygen at the time of exercise. 3. Lactic acid.

3.3 Training methods

LEARNING SUMMARY	**After studying this section you should be able to understand:**
	• a number of training methods
	• the advantages of these training methods
	• the nature of exercise programmes

There is a wide range of different training methods and all are effective to some extent. All place an emphasis on a number of the fitness components on page 29. All of them train both the **aerobic** and **anaerobic** systems.

Differing training methods

AQA	✓
EDEXCEL	✓
OCR	✓
WJEC	✓
CCEA	✓

Aerobic training

Aerobic training should be moderately **strenuous** and **prolonged**. It is carried out at approximately the **TTR level** and uses the **larger** muscle groups. Its effects on the body are that...

- **breathing** is improved – breaths become deeper and fuller
- the **chest size** increases
- the size of the heart increases – this is called **bradycardia**
- the **circulation** improves as more red blood cells become available for work
- the **aerobic threshold** is raised, which improves **endurance** and **cardiovascular fitness**
- the **lung capacity** increases, which brings about a **lower resting** heart rate
- the risk of **cardiovascular disease** is reduced.

Anaerobic training

Anaerobic training should be **very strenuous** and done in **short bursts**. It is carried out above the TTR level and should be undertaken with caution. This type of training includes **rest and recovery periods**.

Its effects on the body are that...

- the **anaerobic threshold** is raised
- muscle size is increased – this is called **hypertrophy**
- muscular **strength** is improved
- the **tolerance** to lactic acid is improved
- the body develops the ability to use its **fat stores** for energy.

Figure 3.3 Aerobic and anaerobic work

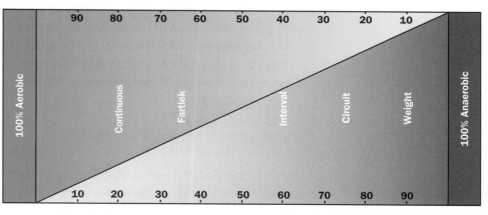

Interval training

Interval training involves alternate periods of high intensity work with rest periods. The rest periods may be inactive, when the body stops moving, or may consist of work at a low intensity. Examples of interval training are:

- For swimming, ten 50-metre sprints with a 20-second total rest between each leg.
- For running, ten 100-metre sprints with a 300-metre jog between each sprint.

With this type of training there are **four** ways in which stress levels can be increased:

- By increasing the speed of the sprint
- By increasing the number of sprints
- By increasing the distance sprinted
- By decreasing the rest periods.

The advantage of interval training is that it is easy to measure progress and improvement.

> Rest periods allow for recovery from oxygen debt.

> These are examples of overload.

Continuous training (LSD training)

Continuous training is also known as LSD training (long, slow, distance training). It involves working for a prolonged period of time at a steady stress level. The intensity of the work will be just below the point where an **oxygen debt** would develop. At the start of the programme an individual may work for only 20 or 30 minutes. However, over a number of sessions, the time spent would increase, although the workload would probably remain the same.

In order to increase the load, the level of intensity can be raised and / or the distance run increased. There are **no** rest periods during this method of training. Improvements should be seen in improved aerobic fitness, increases in the metabolic rate and decreases in percentage of body fat.

> This is the training threshold rate.

> **KEY POINT**
>
> The LSD method is suitable for long-distance swimmers, runners and cyclists as it develops stamina more than speed.

Advantages of this method of training are that it requires very little equipment, it is good for aerobic fitness and it is often easy to do.

Fartlek training

Fartlek training takes its name from a type of training developed in Scandinavia. The word really means '**speed play**', which describes the way the method works.

Fartlek training is very similar to continuous training but includes short, sharp bursts of effort at a much higher intensity, which may be influenced by the terrain or the disposition of the runner. These may be of only 5 or 10 seconds' duration but may well occur every 2 or 3 minutes. If the high level of work lasts for longer than this then an oxygen debt may develop. If this takes place then intensive work is repeated less frequently. Rest periods are included.

> **KEY POINT**
>
> Oxygen debt is replaced during low-level work.

To increase the load, the work periods can be extended or their intensity increased. This type of training can improve both aerobic and anaerobic fitness, increase the metabolic rate and reduce the percentage of body fat.

Advantages of this type of training are that it can be easily adapted to suit the individual, and it reflects the pattern of games that have a regular change of pace, such as football and hockey.

Circuit training

This type of training includes a number of physical activities performed one after the other in the form of a circle or circuit. There are two basic variations: **fixed load** and **individual load**. Both follow a similar pattern.

Fixed load – the individual attempts to perform each exercise continuously over a given time. When this target time is achieved, the circuit is redesigned to increase the stress level by setting a new target (e.g. lengthening the work periods).

Individual load – the individual establishes their own level of work for each exercise. This is usually between 50% and 60% of the maximum that a person can do for one minute of the exercise. They are then timed for each circuit of exercises and aim to be faster each time they do the circuit. With individual load circuits, it is possible to increase stress by reducing the rest periods between the exercises and by increasing the load level.

The order of events is most important.

Circuits can be designed to build up strength, local muscular endurance or total stamina. Figure 3.4 is an example of a simple six-station circuit. Note that each exercise puts stress on a different part of the body and that each body part is worked in turn.

Figure 3.4 A simple six-station circuit

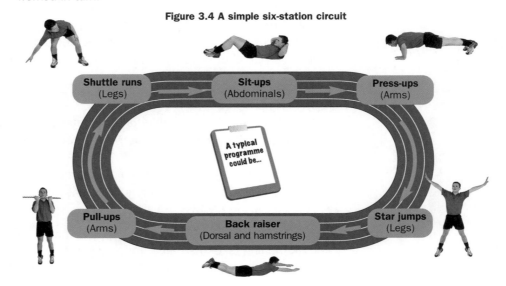

Shuttle runs (Legs) → Sit-ups (Abdominals) → Press-ups (Arms)

A typical programme could be...

Pull-ups (Arms) — Back raiser (Dorsal and hamstrings) — Star jumps (Legs)

The effects of this type of training are that strength, endurance, muscle tone and skill level can be improved. Bone density and metabolic rate increase and body fat percentage decreases.

Advantages of this type of training include...
- boredom is prevented as lots of different exercises are done
- it is not generally affected by the weather as exercises are mainly done inside
- any kind of exercises can be included
- it is easy to measure progress.

Weight training

Weight training can be very similar to circuit training. An individual will complete a set of exercises in a prescribed order using weights, rather than doing a range of different activities. Each station will concentrate on a different part of the body. As training progresses, the weights can be made heavier and rest periods can be reduced.

> **KEY POINT**
>
> The number of times that a weight is lifted is called repetitions or reps. The number of times that a number of reps is repeated is called a set.

As a general rule, it is agreed that, in order to increase strength, a person should lift heavy weights, but with few reps. To increase stamina, light weights should be lifted, but with a large number of reps. An example of a weights circuit is shown in Figure 3.5.

Figure 3.5 Example of a weight training programme

Exercise	Main Muscle Groups Under Stress
Bench press	Chest, front of shoulder, back of upper arm
Front squat	Thigh, hip
Two hands curl	Front of upper arm
Deep knee bend	Legs, back, chest
Side to side bend	Sides of trunk, stomach
Heel lift	Lower leg, ankle

EACH EXERCISE TO BE COMPLETED FIVE TIMES; EACH SET OF EXERCISES TO BE COMPLETED TWICE.
To increase **INTENSITY** the size of the weights used in each activity would be increased.
To increase **DURATION** the number of sets of exercises would be increased.
To increase **FREQUENCY** the number of sessions would be increased.
In this type of activity the individual should start with easily manageable weights and progress to heavier weights gradually.

Figure 3.5 (cont.)

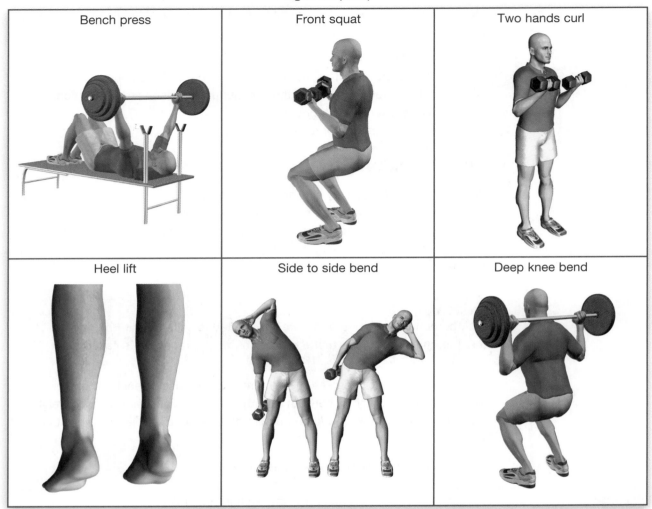

| Bench press | Front squat | Two hands curl |
| Heel lift | Side to side bend | Deep knee bend |

> **Make sure you can explain the difference between isometric and isotonic contractions.**

It must be remembered that there are two main variations of weight training: **isometric weight training** and **isotonic weight training**.

Isometric weight training involves lifting the weight and holding the muscular contraction for up to 5 seconds, then relaxing before repeating the exercise. This means that the overload of the muscle is taking place when the contracted muscle fibres **stay still**. They remain at the contracted length – they do not move. This type of contraction develops strength rather than endurance. Examples of this strength work can be seen during the initial pushing phase of a rugby scrum and during a tug-of-war event.

Isotonic weight training involves raising and lowering the weights repeatedly and rapidly. This means that muscle overload is taking place as the muscle fibres **move**: they are continually shortening and lengthening. This type of contraction develops stamina as well as strength.

The effects of weight training are improvements in muscular strength, muscular endurance, muscle tone and posture. Weight training can also increase muscle size, bone density and metabolic rate.

Advantages of weight training are that it is often a fast way to build up strength, it can be adapted to suit most sports and it can easily be carried out on multi-station weight machines.

Table 3.2 Fitness components most affected by different training methods

	Interval	Continuous	Fartlek	Circuit	Weight
Strength				✓	✓
Speed	✓		✓		
Stamina		✓	✓	✓	✓
Suppleness	✓				
Power	✓				
Agility				✓	✓
Aerobic capacity		✓	✓	✓	
Anaerobic capacity	✓		✓	✓	✓

PROGRESS CHECK

1 Which weight training exercise improves the muscles at the front of the upper arm?
2 Give another name for LSD training.

1. Two-handed curl. 2. Continuous training.

3.4 Exercise programmes

LEARNING SUMMARY

After studying this section you should be able to understand:

- the different types of exercise programmes
- the advantages of different exercise programmes

Exercise programmes

AQA	✓
EDEXCEL	✓
OCR	✓
WJEC	✓
CCEA	✓

You should know about these programmes along with the training methods already learned.

Although, strictly speaking, they are not training methods, there are a number of **exercise programmes** that are of benefit to the individual. These all, to some extent, **promote fitness**, stress the **fun aspect** of performing exercise and concentrate on a number of specific **fitness components**. Most tend not to need a large amount of equipment.

Pressure training

Pressure training is often related to a **particular skill**, such as passing in netball or heading in football. Once a person has **learned** the skill of passing, the skill should be practised in a **pressure situation**, for example, the player now has to pass a number of balls that are fed to him in turn at an increasingly rapid pace. The player finds that he has to adjust to each passing situation quickly. If the balls are fed too quickly or the player becomes fatigued, the skill might well break down. A drill for pressure passing is shown in Figure 3.6.

Figure 3.6 Pressure passing drill

PLAYER

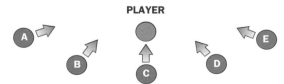

The effect of this type of work is that a skill is done in a game situation rather than in isolation. It is useful in both contact and non-contact sports. The advantage is that it quickly shows a person's ability to perform specific skills in a game situation.

Aerobics

Aerobics is a form of exercise devised to develop **cardiovascular fitness**. Its main aims are to improve muscle tone and reduce the percentage of body fat. It consists mainly of continuous **aerobic exercises**, which follow a set pattern, and it is performed **without equipment**. People often work with a **musical accompaniment** and classes can be either small or very large. The classes are held under the direction of a leader. Rest periods are included and reflect both the intensity of the session and the level of performance of the group.

This type of activity is carried out at **below the TTR** so, usually, no oxygen debt develops. It includes a social element, which encourages participation, with everybody performing the same exercise at the same time.

The advantage of this type of work is that the level of work can be easily adjusted to suit a specific group whilst still providing improvement for the individual.

Step aerobics

Step aerobics is closely related to aerobics, but it includes a single piece of equipment: a portable step.

The step is free-standing, approachable from any side and exercises all include stepping on and off the step within a given routine. Classes are held under the direction of a leader, often with musical accompaniment, with everybody working in unison.

The intensity levels can be adjusted not only by the speed of the steps, but also by raising the step to double height. The lifting of one's own body weight can be very demanding.

Aqua aerobics

Aqua aerobics is another aerobics-related activity, but it takes place in a swimming pool. Exercises are similar to those of the conventional aerobics sessions, but with the constraints that water puts on the individual. The water acts in two ways: firstly as a resistance, making the movement of a body part more difficult than in a normal setting; secondly, it acts as a measure of support for those people who are overweight or are recovering from illness or injury.

Exercises are leader-led from the pool side to the accompaniment of music. Group dynamics influence progress and give support.

Pilates

Pilates is a body-conditioning programme of exercises that mainly includes **stretching and mobility work** and some **static** isometric strength exercises. The level of intensity means that it is most often well below the TTR level, and **injuries rarely occur**.

Exercises are leader-led with the group all performing at the same time, thereby giving each other moral support.

Pilates combines **physical work** with a **philosophical approach** to exercise. This helps to promote a '**feel good**', '**look good**' factor.

Yoga

Yoga is also a conditioning programme that aims to **unify** physical performance with a mental approach.

Yoga includes a series of **passive stretching activities** combined with **mobility** work and some **static strength** work. Activities are leader-led but within a quiet contemplative atmosphere.

Progress is achieved by progressing through carefully **structured** intensity levels, which aim to improve vitality, stamina, posture, strength and weight reduction.

Flexibility training

The body's flexibility can be improved by carrying out a series of mobility exercises for the joints. Each joint should be exercised in turn and can be stretched or moved to just beyond its **point of resistance**. For improvement to take place, the stretch should be held for 8–10 seconds, and the mobility exercises should be carried out for at least 10 minutes. To be fully effective, the mobility exercises should be carried out approximately three times per week.

There are two main types of flexibility exercises: **static** and **ballistic**.

A **static stretching exercise** involves moving the joint to beyond its point of resistance and holding the position still for 8–10 seconds. This can be done in either a **passive** or an **active** manner. Passive stretching is when a partner forces the performer to stretch the joint; active stretching is when the performer forces the joint on his own (see Figure 3.7).

Figure 3.7 Active and passive static stretching

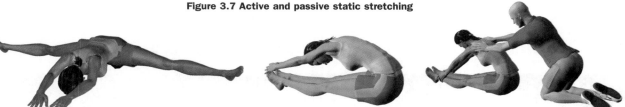

Ballistic stretching uses the momentum of the body or a body part at a joint. Exercises such as arm swinging, bouncing, twisting and turning are ballistic moves (see Figure 3.8).

Take great care with ballistic exercises. They should be attempted only by people with a good degree of flexibility.

Figure 3.8 Ballistic stretching

Advantages of flexibility training are that...

- it is **cheap and easy** to do
- **little equipment** is needed
- exercises can be done alone
- not a lot of space is needed
- it supports the playing of a **wide range** of activities.

PROGRESS CHECK

1. Explain the term 'Fartlek'.
2. Explain how weight training exercises should be performed to increase strength.
3. Explain the difference between active stretch and passive stretch.
4. Explain the difference between isometric and isotonic contractions.

1. 'Fartlek' means 'speed play' – running with a repeated change of pace.
2. Use heavy weights with a low number of reps.
3. Active stretch is done alone; passive stretch is done with a partner.
4. In an isometric contraction the muscle fibres stay the same length and the load is held still. In an isotonic contraction the load is moved and the static fibres contract and relax.

3.5 Training requirements

LEARNING SUMMARY

After studying this section you should be able to understand:

- the different parts of a training session and the value of rest periods
- the short-term and long-term effects of training
- the planning needs of a training programme

Parts of a training session

AQA	✓
EDEXCEL	✓
OCR	✓
WJEC	✓
CCEA	✓

Training sessions should be interesting, useful and suitable. A range of different activities will prevent **boredom**, the activities must be seen to be **useful and suitable**, taking account of age, injuries, fitness levels and physical abilities. As with all training programmes, the training session must be structured. It must include a warm-up, the training activity and a cool down.

KEY POINT

Keep to the order: warm up ➡ training activities ➡ cool down / rest.

The warm-up

> You must be able to construct a warm-up session.

A **warm-up** is essential – you should never attempt a training session without a warm-up. It should include a number of exercises that will gradually get the whole body **ready for work**. Warm-up exercises must...

- raise the **blood flow** to the muscles (i.e. your pulse will be raised)
- include **stretching** exercises to prepare the joints and muscles for the harder work
- raise the **body temperature** and prepare the mind for the physical work ahead.

It is essential that this work **complements** the main part of the session. This work is necessary if injury is to be avoided during training.

The training activity

The **training activity** can take many forms. The exercises should be **varied** and should **relate** to the sport that you are training for.

Prolonged work on a small number of exercises can become boring and the effects of the training will then be reduced. When choosing exercises it is important to remember the **principles** of overload, progression, specificity and reversibility described in Chapter 2 (see page 33). **Skill** work should be included – both learning new skills and practising known skills individually, in groups, and in conditioned play situations, as well as in the full game situation.

The cool down

Make sure you are able to explain the value of the cool down.

The **cool down** is important as it helps to get your body back to normal, to its steady state. When a hard physical training session ends, a large supply of blood is retained in the muscles. This should be returned to general circulation as soon as possible to avoid **pooling**. If pooling does develop this can contribute to a feeling of faintness and dizziness. It is important to get rid of any **oxygen debt** that might have developed and to flush out any **residual lactic acid**. The type of exercises to be included in the cool down should be similar to those in the warm-up, but should gradually decrease in intensity.

Rest periods

Rest periods are as important to training as hard physical exercise. During intensive repeated periods of physical work, **muscle fibres** may become slightly **damaged** and develop a shortage of **glycogen**. The inclusion of rest days when only light training or no physical work is done will allow the muscles to recover naturally.

> **KEY POINT**
>
> Rest days or light training days are most important just before competition. They allow the body to enter competition fully prepared.

Effects of training

AQA	✓
EDEXCEL	✓
OCR	✓
WJEC	✓
CCEA	✓

For training to be effective, it must last over a long period of time. However, training exercises also have immediate **short-term** effects (see Table 3.3).

Make sure you are able to differentiate between long- and short-term effects.

Table 3.3 Short-term effects of exercise

Effect	Reason
Increased breathing rate	More oxygen needed for muscles to work, helps body to stay cool
Rise in pulse rate	Transports more oxygen to muscles and removes waste materials, i.e. CO_2
Sweating	Helps body to stay cool
Going red	Blood moves to just below skin surface to radiate heat outwards and help to keep the body cool
Blood diverted from other organs	Diverted to muscles that are working hard
Rise in body temperature	This is a by-product of the muscles working hard.

Prolonged training has a number of effects on various body parts (see Table 3.4).

Table 3.4 Long-term effects of training

Body part	Effect
Heart	• Range increases, increases slightly in size, stroke volume (i.e. blood forced out by each beat of the heart) increases
Lungs	• Maximal inspiratory and expiratory levels increase, more alveoli are ready for work • Increase in capillary beds in alveoli
Chest	• Increases in size • Ability to expand increases
Muscles	• Get shorter and fatter • More muscle fibres are ready for work • Blood supply improves
Skeleton	• Bones become stronger • Flexibility increases

KEY POINT

Overall, the body will become stronger, more flexible, able to withstand greater stress and will recover more quickly from hard physical activity.

Temperature control

Training at any level can bring about a rise in the core temperature of the body. In order to maintain the body at around 37°C...

- the blood vessels under the skin **vasodilate** (i.e. get bigger)
- the **shunt** vessel systems adapt to needs
- the skin's surface becomes red as heat is **radiated** outwards
- the sweat glands **release** sweat to help the cooling process
- heavy breathing (**panting**) brings cool air into the body and passes hot air out.

Figure 3.9 Operation of shunt mechanism

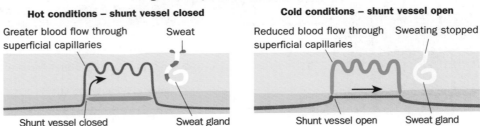

Hot conditions – shunt vessel closed	Cold conditions – shunt vessel open
Greater blood flow through superficial capillaries Sweat	Reduced blood flow through superficial capillaries Sweating stopped
Shunt vessel closed Sweat gland	Shunt vessel open Sweat gland

The training programme

AQA ✓
EDEXCEL ✓
OCR ✓
WJEC ✓
CCEA ✓

A training programme must meet the needs of the performer and relate to the game or activity that the individual is training for. It should be carefully planned to be carried out over a prolonged period of time. This planning should aim to achieve climax at competition time and take into account the close season of any activity.

There are **four** stages that should be followed:

Remember SPIRe:
S = Suitability;
P = Preparation;
I = In-season;
Re = Recuperation

❶ Suitability for training – Individuals must ensure that they are capable of following a sustained training programme. They must be free from injury and illness, have access to training facilities and have a genuine desire to improve their performance.

Figure 3.10 Seasonal sport

Key

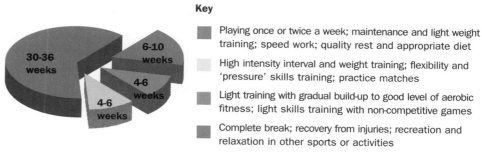

Playing once or twice a week; maintenance and light weight training; speed work; quality rest and appropriate diet

High intensity interval and weight training; flexibility and 'pressure' skills training; practice matches

Light training with gradual build-up to good level of aerobic fitness; light skills training with non-competitive games

Complete break; recovery from injuries; recreation and relaxation in other sports or activities

2 **Preparation – Off-season / out-of-season** training should concentrate on maintaining a basic fitness level, attaining the correct body weight for the activity and include the acquisition of any required skills. **Pre-season training** should include developing the energy systems, both aerobic and anaerobic work, developing strength and practising team-play situations.

3 **In-season training – Competition training** should aim to maintain fitness and skill levels and fluctuate in degrees of intensity so that the performer can peak at different times throughout the season as major events occur. Training should rise to a peak, then be followed by rest days just before competitions.

4 **Recuperation – Post-season training** should not be overlooked. At the end of the competitive season it is essential that the performer continues with a light training programme to allow the body to recover from the stresses and strains of the season. It is at this time that more serious injuries should be dealt with prior to the start of off-season work.

Year-round sports

Many performers now look to compete at a number of venues around the world, turning their sport into an all-year activity. To meet the demands of this type of competition, elite performers tend to train in warmer weather and often at high altitude. Funding for this is often self-financed or comes from sponsorship or grants. However, training must still be organised with short-, medium- and long-term goals. Specific peaks of performance are planned for and training is organised into blocks of time. This is called periodisation. The goals might be a four-year aim of an Olympic event or specific events within a 12-month period. At each event, the performer will expect to improve on the level of performance, still looking for the ultimate long-term goal.

> You should be able to describe a training programme for a sport that you know.

Figure 3.11 Periodisation peaks

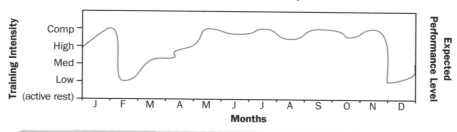

PROGRESS CHECK

1 Give two reasons for warming-up before starting physical activity.

2 What are the main parts of a training session?

3 What is 'blood pooling' and when might it occur?

1. To prepare the mind and body; To increase blood supply to the muscles. **2.** Warm-up, training activity and cool down. **3.** The concentration of blood left in the muscles if no cool-down period takes place after hard physical work.

Sample GCSE questions

1   Maria wants to improve her cardiovascular endurance.

   (a)   Should she train aerobically or anaerobically to achieve this?

      Aerobically   **(1)**

   (b)   Which of the following is the most appropriate training method she should use to improve her cardiovascular endurance: weight training, interval or continuous?

      Continuous   **(1)** ◄   **Continuous training is also referred to as LSD.**

   (c)   What is the purpose of ATP?

      It supplies the muscles with energy.   **(2)** ◄   **Remember that two facts are needed, as two marks are available – muscles and energy.**

   (d)   What does pyruvic acid turn into if oxygen is present?

      Water (H_2O) and Carbon dioxide (CO_2)   **(2)** ◄   **Again, two marks are available so two facts are expected in your answer.**

2   A training session should always finish with a cool down.

   (a)   Give **two** examples of activities that might be included in a cool down.

      Jogging / Walking, Stretching.   **(2)** ◄   **Jogging and walking are really very similar. Try to give two very different activities, e.g. jogging and stretching.**

   (b)   **(i)**   Give **two** physical reasons why you should cool down at the end of a training session.

      To maintain circulation, remove lactic acid, aid the delivery of oxygen and re-stretch muscles after work.   **(2)**

      (ii)   Explain why the reasons you have given above are important.

      To prevent fainting, dizziness and blood pooling; To reduce the chance of lactic acid build-up; To prevent muscle stiffness.   **(2)**

◄   **Although there are a number of possible answers, you only need to give two. Extra answers will not gain extra marks. Also, you will need to link this part of the question with part (ii).**

Exam practice questions

1 What does the shunt vessel system help to control?

.... **(1)**

2 Give **two** features of Fartlek training.

(a) ....

(b) .... **(2)**

3 List the **two** main types of flexibility exercises.

(a) ....

(b) .... **(2)**

4 (a) What does 'TTR' stand for?

....

(b) Explain how to calculate TTR using the 180 method.

....

....

....

....

.... **(4)**

5 List the correct order in which six activities might be included in a simple circuit.

....

....

....

....

....

.... **(6)**

4 Skill

The following topics are covered in this chapter:

- **Types of skill**
- **Information processing models**
- **Contribution to performance**

4.1 Types of skill

LEARNING SUMMARY

After studying this section you should be able to understand:

- the term 'skill' and the difference between types of skills
- how skills are learned
- the basic nervous system
- the basic information processing models

Skill defined

AQA	✗
EDEXCEL	✗
OCR	✓
WJEC	✓
CCEA	✓

One of the best definitions of skill is: 'the **learned** ability to bring about **pre-determined** results with maximum certainty, often with the **minimum outlay** of time, or energy, or both'. The important parts of this definition are:

- **Learned** – a skill is something that is learned. Although some people seem to perform a skill naturally, all physical skills have to be learned.
- **Pre-determined** – a skill has a result that is anticipated. The outcome of a skill action is expected by the performer.
- **Minimum outlay** – a skill learned correctly is performed with the minimum of effort. It is a skill that uses the components of fitness efficiently. There is a control of physical movement.

> **KEY POINT**
>
> Skill is learned, has a predetermined outcome, and involves the minimum outlay of effort.

Types of skills

AQA	✗
EDEXCEL	✗
OCR	✓
WJEC	✓
CCEA	✓

Basic and complex skills

Basic skills are physical skills that...

- are learned at an early age
- are easily transferred to a number of situations, for example, running in different ways, throwing for height or distance
- form the basis for more complex skills, for example, the swivel hips on the trampoline combines the basic seat drop with a basic twisting movement.

Complex skills are physical skills that...

- are specific to a given sport, for example, a serve in tennis
- need a considerable amount of practice to learn correctly, due to the number of basic skills that are linked together.

In tennis, for example, the serve is a complex skill, made up of a number of basic skills: holding the racket correctly; being able to throw a ball in the air correctly; being able to hit something above your head correctly; and being able to direct the ball to a specific point when you hit it. All these basic skills have to be learned and practised before they can be put together to produce the complex skill of serving.

Open and closed skills

Skills are often described as the amount of control that the individual has over the timing of the performance. This is called **pacing**. In some situations, like the tennis serve, the performer will have full control of when the skill will be performed. This is **internal pacing** or **self pacing**. The player decides when to serve. In other situations, like paddling a canoe down a white water slalom course, external forces will affect when the paddling skill has to be performed. This is **external pacing**. Rocks and waves will decide when the canoeist will paddle.

Pacing has a bearing on whether a skill is described as an **open** or **closed** skill:
- **Open** skills are most influenced by external factors, e.g. deciding when to perform a tackle in a football or a hockey game depends as much on the actions of other players as on the ability to tackle.
- **Closed** skills follow a set, predetermined pattern of movement regardless of any external factors, e.g. the archer, not his target, decides when to fire the arrow.

Some skills may be part-open and part-closed. A forehand in badminton falls into both categories: it depends on your opponent hitting the shuttle to you (an external influence), but you decide whether to play the shot early or late. All skills will fall somewhere along the line of the skill pendulum (see Figure 4.1).

Figure 4.1 The skill pendulum

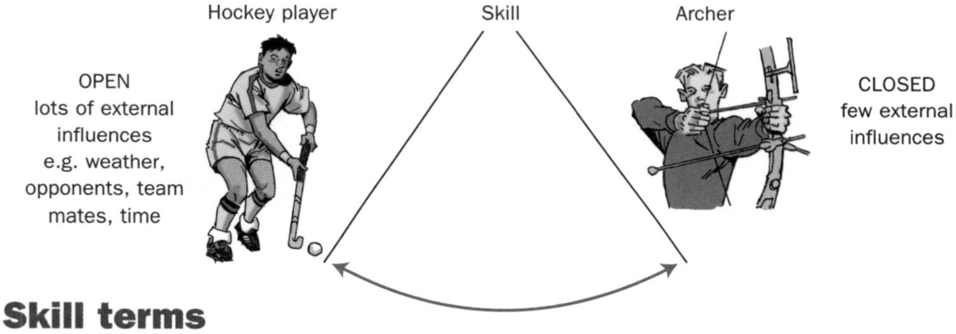

OPEN lots of external influences e.g. weather, opponents, team mates, time

CLOSED few external influences

Skill terms

Motor skills describe skills associated with muscle action. Fine motor skills use precise, delicate movements, such as picking up an egg. **Gross** motor skills use large muscle groups in actions such as discus throwing.

Perceptual motor skills often describe externally paced open skills in which the interpretation of sensory information takes place. An example would be how to react in order to catch a ball.

Fundamental motor skills describe the motor skills of running, throwing, jumping, catching and hitting.

Cognitive skills are those that require the use of **problem-solving** and reasoning. They include working out **tactics** in a game situation or changing performance after a trial and error process. If an opponent can always return a backhand serve in tennis with ease, then a change to a forehand serve might be more effective. It is not the serve, but the process of decision-making that is cognitive.

Make sure you can break down complex skills from your chosen sports.

You must be able to differentiate between open and closed skills.

It is essential to be able to analyse these basic skills within a wide range of physical activities.

Learning skills

AQA	X
EDEXCEL	X
OCR	✓
WJEC	✓
CCEA	✓

Skill acquisition

The main ways in which skills are learned or acquired are as follows:

- **As a whole** – you repeat the skill as one exercise without breaking it into parts. For example, dribbling in football does not lend itself to being split into parts.
- **In parts** – the skill is broken down into manageable parts. Each part is learned and then all the parts are put together. For example, in a tennis serve, you must learn...
  - to throw the ball up correctly
  - how to grip the racket
  - the correct foot position
  - how to transfer weight from your back foot to your front foot
  - how to swing the racket
  - when to hit the ball
  - with which part of the racket head to hit the ball.
- By **fixed practice** – a closed skill is repeated time and again, regardless of the environmental conditions. For example, a golfer will practise hitting a ball off the tee in all weather conditions.
- By **variable practice** – this is when an open skill is learned and practised. For example, a soccer player will learn to kick a ball on long and short grass, in the wind and in the rain, etc.
- By **rehearsal** – practising of the movement pattern 'in theory', for example, practising the tennis serve action without actually hitting the ball.
- By **observation, trial and error** – attempting to copy an observed skill, possibly from a highly skilled performer. Each repeated performance of the skill can be adjusted to correct any errors. For example, when shooting an arrow, the action can be altered until the centre of the target is hit.

Guidance

Guidance is the help that a person receives when learning a new skill. It comes in three forms:

1. **Visual** – You **watch** the skill first, by demonstration, video or from a series of pictures in a book, which gives you a **clear image** of what is required. You then try to **repeat**, or mimic, what you have seen. A skilled performance can be recorded and **played back** so that the performer can see the parts of the skill being performed correctly and the parts being performed incorrectly.

2. **Verbal** – A teacher or a coach may **explain** the skill to you, highlighting the main aspects. You then try to perform the skill remembering the important points.

3. **Manual** – It is possible for a teacher or coach to **put** the performer in the correct position for the performance of the skill. The body and muscles get a feel of what the skilled performance is like. When this **muscle memory** is learned, it should make the performance more successful. For example, if a performer's body is held in the correct position for a handstand, the body should remember this and help the performer to replicate this position when repeated attempts are made.

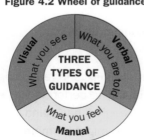

Figure 4.2 Wheel of guidance

4.2 Information processing models

LEARNING SUMMARY	**After studying this section you should be able to understand:**
	• the nervous system
	• basic information processing models and their contribution to performance

The nervous system

AQA	X
EDEXCEL	X
OCR	X
WJEC	✓
CCEA	✓

All movement is controlled by the **nervous system** of the body. This is made up of...

- the **brain**
- the **brain stem**
- the **spinal cord**
- **nerves**, often called **neurones**.

The brain, the brain stem and the spinal cord are collectively called the **Central Nervous System (CNS)**. It is in these parts that all decisions are made. The nerves that branch out from the CNS are often called the **Peripheral Nervous System** (see Figure 4.3).

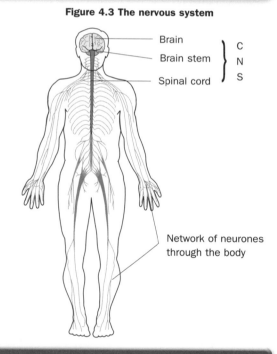

Figure 4.3 The nervous system

Brain
Brain stem   C N S
Spinal cord

Network of neurones through the body

Acting on information received

AQA	X
EDEXCEL	X X
OCR	X
WJEC	✓
CCEA	✓

There are two basic types of nerve:

- **Sensory nerves** – these carry information to the CNS.
- **Effector nerves** – these carry information away from the CNS.

Sensory nerves carry **afferent** nerve impulses **to** the CNS: these are sometimes called **afferent nerves**.

Effector nerves carry **efferent** nerve impulses **away** from the CNS: these are also known as **efferent nerves** or **motor nerves**.

> It is essential that you can distinguish between the two types of nerve, and that you know the names for each type of nerve.

You should know the difference between exterioceptors, proprioceptors and interioceptors.

Sensory nerves obtain information from outside the body via **exterioceptors**, such as the ears, eyes and skin. They also obtain information from within the body from **proprioceptors**, such as the stretch receptors of muscles. **Interioceptors** provide information on the internal state of the body, such as how fast the heart is beating, or how full the bladder is.

The way in which information is received and acted upon follows a set pattern, as shown in Figure 4.4.

Figure 4.4 Information receipt and action pattern

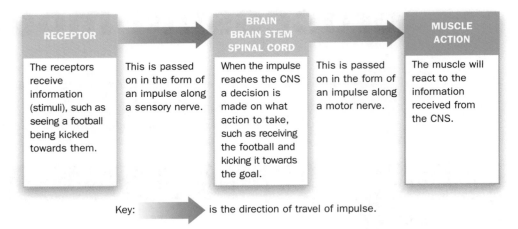

Key: ➤ is the direction of travel of impulse.

The speed at which a decision is made is called the **reaction time**. Knowing **how** to perform a skill is important, but knowing **when** to perform a skill is equally important. For example, as your opponent serves in tennis, you receive lots of information through the eyes and ears, and from within your body. These different types of information are called **stimuli** and they are passed to the CNS before any action is taken.

Remember that the CNS is part of the nervous system.

So, information from outside the body (about your opponent's serve) is detected by the exterioceptors in your eyes and ears. At the same time, the CNS will be receiving stimuli from the proprioceptors within your body. These tell you what position your body is in as you prepare to receive the service. All this received information – the stimuli – is described as the **input**, and any action taken is called the **output**. Once the input has been received, it is necessary to make decisions about **what** the output should be and **when** the output should take place. This process is called the **information processing model** (see Figure 4.5).

Figure 4.5 The simple information processing model

Feedback and performance

You should be aware of the importance of feedback in the information processing model.

The skilled performer will be able to adjust the output as it is being performed or as it is being repeated. This adjustment is often made on the basis of **knowledge of results** or **knowledge of performance**. This is called **feedback**.

If an output has the desired effect, e.g. we hit the target when shooting an arrow, we will try to repeat the same process in order to get the same results. This is called **knowledge of results**. By the same token, we sometimes perform a physical skill and, regardless of its outcome, we know that 'it feels right'. This is called **knowledge of performance**.

Both knowledge of results and knowledge of performance can affect an output (see Figure 4.6).

Figure 4.6 The information processing model

Figure 4.7 The extended information processing model

The interpretation of received stimuli by our brains is called perception. When perception takes place, inputs are checked against known remembered patterns of stimuli before a decision about output is made. This checking is done very quickly in the memory stores of the CNS (see Figure 4.7)

When our senses receive information, we often take in more stimuli than we need to. A professional footballer taking a penalty kick needs to know where the ball is, where the keeper is and where the goal is. He may also be aware of the noise of the crowd and the flashing of cameras. However, since our brains can deal with only a limited amount of stimuli, a selection process takes place. This part of the processing model is called limited channel capacity: some information is allowed through whilst other information is not (see Figure 4.8).

Figure 4.8 Limited channel capacity in the information processing model

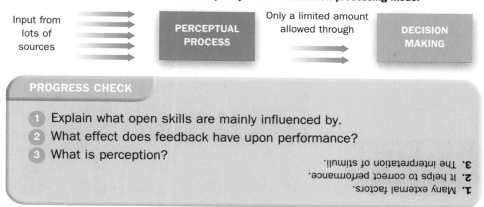

PROGRESS CHECK

1. Explain what open skills are mainly influenced by.
2. What effect does feedback have upon performance?
3. What is perception?

3. The interpretation of stimuli.
2. It helps to correct performance.
1. Many external factors.

4.3 Contribution to performance

LEARNING SUMMARY

After studying this section you should be able to understand:

- the effects of motivation and arousal on performance
- the necessity for goal-setting

Motivation and arousal

AQA	✗
EDEXCEL	✗
OCR	✓
WJEC	✓
CCEA	✓

Motivation

Motivation is the amount of desire or enthusiasm that a person has for a given physical performance. This can influence how well or how badly an individual will perform.

There are two types of motivation:

1 **Intrinsic motivation** – when a person motivates himself / herself. The desire to succeed comes from within.

2 **Extrinsic motivation** – when a person's desire to succeed is stimulated by the chance of winning a trophy or prize. The motivation to succeed comes from outside.

> **KEY POINT**
>
> The examples given above are positive motivations. Negative motivations can hinder performance.

Arousal

Your level of **arousal** can be described as how prepared you are to take part in an event. How keen you are to take part can influence how hard you might try to win. Unfortunately, it is possible to **over-arouse** a competitor. Too much arousal can lead to **anxiety** and excessive **stress**, causing a decrease in performance standards. Figure 4.9 represents the **Inverted U Theory** of arousal.

Figure 4.9 Graph showing arousal level compared to performance level

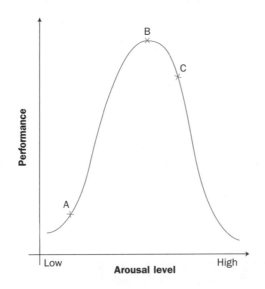

You should be able to explain the Inverted U Theory.

- At point A on the graph there is little arousal and so the performance level is not raised.
- At point B the arousal level is at a middle level and performance is at its best.
- At point C, however, the arousal level has become so high that anxiety and stress are having a negative effect on performance, the standard of which is beginning to decrease. At this stage the performer is said to be 'psyched out'; a person cannot give their best in this situation.

> **PROGRESS CHECK**
>
> **1** Where does intrinsic motivation come from?
> **2** What effect does negative motivation have on performance?
> **3** What effect does excessive stress have on performance?
>
> **3.** It can cause a decrease in performance.
> **2.** It can hinder performance levels.
> **1.** Within the performer.

Sample GCSE questions

1 **(a)** Name a sport, or an action from a sport, and explain why it is self paced.

A handstand in gymnastics - the performer chooses when to perform the action. **(2)**

(b) Name a sport, or an action in a sport, and explain why it is externally paced.

Heading the ball in soccer - the timing of the action is dictated by other players or events. **(2)**

2 Draw and label a diagram to represent the simple information processing model.

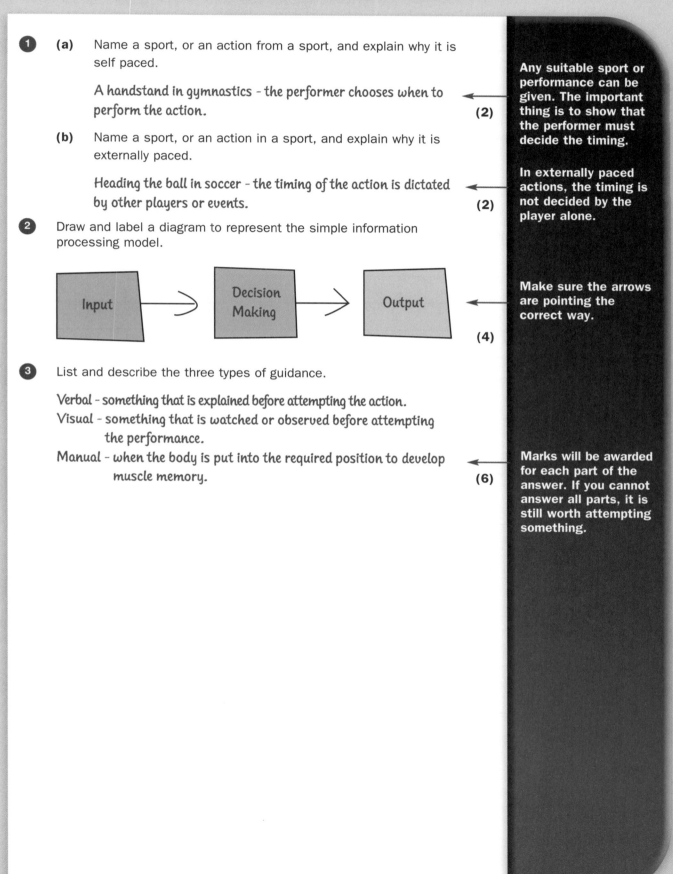

(4)

3 List and describe the three types of guidance.

Verbal - something that is explained before attempting the action.
Visual - something that is watched or observed before attempting the performance.
Manual - when the body is put into the required position to develop muscle memory. **(6)**

Any suitable sport or performance can be given. The important thing is to show that the performer must decide the timing.

In externally paced actions, the timing is not decided by the player alone.

Make sure the arrows are pointing the correct way.

Marks will be awarded for each part of the answer. If you cannot answer all parts, it is still worth attempting something.

Exam practice questions

1 Define reaction time.

....

.... **(2)**

2 Give the names of **two** sports where reaction time is important.

(a) ....

(b) .... **(2)**

3 Give a suitable definition of the term 'skill'.

....

....

....

.... **(6)**

4 Explain the difference between sensory nerves and effector nerves.

....

....

.... **(2)**

5 **(a)** Draw and label a diagram showing the limited channel capacity in the information process.

(b) Explain what happens to some stimuli when they reach this part of the process.

....

.... **(8)**

5 Measurement in sport

The following topics are covered in this chapter:

- **The value of testing**
- **Specific tests**

5.1 The value of testing

LEARNING SUMMARY

After studying this section you should be able to understand:

- why testing takes place in sport and how the data obtained can be used
- how testing takes place in sport

Why test?

AQA ✓
EDEXCEL ✓
OCR ✓
WJEC ✓
CCEA ✓

It can be argued that measurement / testing is taking place in sport at all times. At the most simplistic level this includes counting the **score** in a game like football or badminton. The score shows which individual or team scores most points and is, therefore, the most able. When successive games are played against a number of opponents, then the scores for each game can indicate which individual or team is the most able overall, and whether the individual or team has improved their performance.

On a more complex level, it is possible to measure the effects that specific types of training have on the individual, and to establish, for example, how fit, strong or supple the person is.

> **KEY POINT**
>
> Anything can be tested if the right test is available.

How to test

By testing the individual **before** they start a training programme, it is possible to identify those physical deficiencies that need to be improved in order to attain fitness. Repeated testing can indicate levels of **progression** during a training programme.

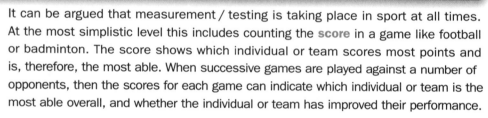
You must know the meanings of the technical terms related to testing.

In all tests it is important to ensure that the test measures what it sets out to measure, for example, a test for arm strength should not include the use of the leg muscles. This is called **validity**.

After a test has been carried out, **results** are obtained. The results of the test are **data**. Data can be illustrated in a graph, bar chart or pie chart and should always be studied closely – this is the **analysis** of the data. By analysing the data, it is possible to draw **conclusions** about, for example, how effective the training programme is, or how strong an individual is compared to another.

Sometimes tests come with a list of **norms**. Norms are sets of figures that indicate, in general terms, how fit, strong or supple an individual might be compared with other people of the same age. Care must be taken when comparing individual scores with norms: such comparisons are very simplified and not definitive.

All tests used should have both proven **objectivity** and **reliability**. For a test to be objective, the results must not reflect the views or attitudes of the tester. For a test to be deemed reliable, the data obtained after one test will be the same as that obtained when the test is repeated on the same individual, either by the same tester or by another tester. Whenever a test is used it should be carried out in the correct way. The correct method for carrying out a test is called **test protocol** and, if it is not followed, the results might be incorrect.

Before embarking on any practical tests, an excellent starting point for any assessment is the use of a **Physical Activity Readiness Questionnaire (PAR-Q)**. Data obtained from this questionnaire can indicate how to proceed with further assessments.

> This warning is very important.

> The person being tested is sometimes called a 'testee'.

KEY POINT

No test should be attempted unless...
- a suitably qualified person is present
- the person being tested is medically fit to take the test
- a suitable warm-up has taken place before testing starts.

Data analysis

Data obtained from any test should indicate the quality of that performance, i.e. how good or poor that person's performance was compared to others who have completed the same test (or compared to that person's previous results).

Although **comparisons** can be made between different people's test results, it should be remembered that any results obtained from physical tests are only an **indication** of the status of the individual. Results can be influenced by many factors, especially protocol. Many performers look to testing not only to compare themselves with other performers but to measure **progress**, or lack of it. (Remember the five principles of fitness discussed in Chapter 2.)

PROGRESS CHECK

1. Explain the following terms: **(a)** Validity **(b)** Data **(c)** Norms **(d)** Protocol.

1. **(a)** The test measures what it sets out to measure. **(b)** Scores obtained from a test. **(c)** Sets of figures (data) that indicate, in general terms, how fit or strong or supple an individual might be, compared with people of the same age. **(d)** The way a test should be carried out.

5.2 Specific tests

LEARNING SUMMARY

After studying this section you should be able to understand:
- tests for strength, suppleness and stamina
- tests for cardiovascular fitness
- tests for skill-related fitness
- combination tests for physical fitness

Tests for strength

AQA ✓
EDEXCEL ✓
OCR ✓
WJEC ✓
CCEA ✓

Figure 5.1 Grip dynamometer

Figure 5.2 Tensiometer

Measuring hand and forearm strength

A **grip dynamometer** is used to test hand and forearm strength. Before using the dynamometer, make sure that the pointer is set at zero. The testee then grips and squeezes as hard as possible (see Figure 5.1). Measurement is taken from the dial.

Measuring leg and back strength

A **tensiometer** is used for measuring leg and back strength. Before using a tensiometer, make sure that the pointer is set on zero. Although this piece of equipment is easy to use, it must be used correctly. When pulling on the handles, your back must be kept upright and straight (see Figure 5.2). Measurement is taken from the dial.

Measuring power

Power is a combination of **speed** and **strength**. Power can be measured in the legs by using either the **standing high jump** or the **standing long jump** tests. These are tests of **explosive** strength (see Figure 5.3 and Figure 5.4).

For the standing high jump, the subject faces the wall and stretches both arms above their head with their hands side by side so that fingertip level whilst standing can be marked. The subject then turns sideways to the wall and, with both feet together, jumps as high as possible to touch the board with the fingertips of one outstretched hand. (The subject may swing arms before jumping if desired.) The distance jumped is the distance between the two marks.

For the standing long jump, the subject stands on a non-slip surface, usually a gymnastics mat, marked with a straight line. The subject performs a two-footed jump forwards along the mat. (The subject may swing their arms before jumping if desired.) The distance jumped is measured from the start line to the back of the rearmost heel (see Figure 5.4).

Figure 5.3 Standing high jump

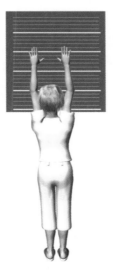

Figure 5.4 Standing long jump

Tests for suppleness

AQA	✓
EDEXCEL	✓
OCR	✓
WJEC	✓
CCEA	✓

Tests for suppleness tend to be localised, i.e. they measure suppleness for only **one part** of the body.

The shoulder lift

The shoulder lift test measures flexibility at the shoulder joint (see Figure 5.5). The subject lies face down on the floor and grasps the short stick in each hand with hands shoulder-width apart. The short stick is raised as high as possible with the arms straight and the chin touching the ground. The height that the stick is raised from the ground is the measurement of shoulder suppleness:

Rating for shoulder lift (cm): 36+ = very good; 25+ = good; 20+ = fair; 15+ = poor.

The sit-and-reach test

The sit-and-reach test measures suppleness in the back and hamstrings (see Figure 5.6). The subject sits on the floor with their legs fully extended, feet flexed and hands touching the sit-and-reach box. The subject stretches forward with both hands (keeping legs straight) and slides their palms along the box. The distance the fingertips reach beyond the toes is the measurement. If the subject cannot reach beyond the toes, the distance from the fingertips to the toes is measured. This is a negative score. The subject must **not** jerk forward, but stretch forward in an even manner.

Rating for sit-and-reach (cm): 10+ = very good; 5+ = good; 0+ = fair; <5 = poor.

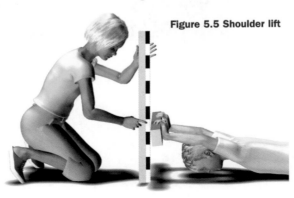

Figure 5.5 Shoulder lift

Figure 5.6 Sit-and-reach test

Trunk extension

This test measures the suppleness of the lower back (see Figure 5.7). The subject lies face down on the floor with both hands clasped behind their head. The head and shoulders are raised as high as possible, whilst the feet remain in contact with the ground. The measurement is the distance from the floor to the point of the chin.

Rating for trunk extension (cm): 50+ = very good; 40+ = good; 30+ = fair; 20+ = poor.

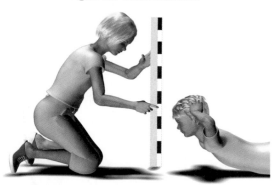

Figure 5.7 Trunk extension

Tests for stamina

AQA	✓
EDEXCEL	✓
OCR	✓
WJEC	✓
CCEA	✓

The following tests are for **local muscular stamina**. They test specific muscle groups.

Press-ups

Press-ups measure arm and body strength (see Figure 5.8). Press-ups should always be completed with the back straight. Sometimes, people with reduced arm strength adjust the front support position and pivot round the knees rather than the feet. Even so, the back must be kept straight. Measurement is the maximum number of press-ups completed.

Sit-ups

Sit-ups measure the strength and endurance of the abdominal muscles (see Figure 5.9). The subject lies flat on their back on a mat with their hands clasped behind their head. Knees should be at right angles, and both feet flat on the floor and slightly apart. The subject sits up to touch their knees with their elbows and then returns to starting position. A partner holds the subject's ankles to make sure their feet stay on the floor. Measurement is the total number of sit-ups completed in 30 seconds.

Rating for sit-ups: 25+ = very good; 20+ = good; 16+ = fair; 14+ = poor.

Figure 5.8 Press-ups

Figure 5.9 Sit-ups

Pull-ups / chins

Pull-ups (chins) measure the strength and endurance of the upper arm, especially the biceps and the shoulder girdle (see Figure 5.10). The subject holds a pair of rings (as shown) or a beam, using the underhand grip, with feet clear of the floor. The chin is then raised above the beam and then the arms are fully extended. Measurement is the number of times the chin is raised above the beam, or rings, after a **full arm extension**.

Ratings for pull-ups:
Males: 13+ = excellent; 9+ = good; 6+ = average; 3+ = fair; <3 = poor.
Females: 6+ = excellent; 5+ = good; 3+ = average; 1+ = fair; 0 = poor.

Figure 5.10 Pull-ups (chins)

Dips

Dips measure the strength and endurance of the upper arm, especially the triceps and the shoulder girdle (see Figure 5.11). The subject supports their full body weight on both hands with their arms fully extended. The hands are placed on suitable bars shoulder-width apart. The body is lowered until the elbows bend to 90 degrees. The arms are then fully extended. The measurement is the number of dips followed by a full arm extension.

Ratings for dips:
Males: 15+ = good; 7–14 = average; <6 = poor.
N.B. Females do not usually do this test.

Figure 5.11 Dips

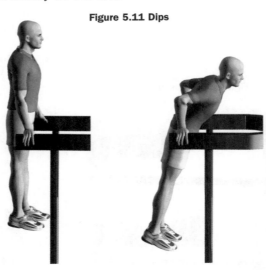

Cardiovascular fitness

AQA	✓
EDEXCEL	✓
OCR	✓
WJEC	✓
CCEA	✓

Cardiovascular fitness is often referred to as **cardiovascular stamina**, **cardiovascular endurance**, **aerobic power** or **aerobic capacity**.

Cardiovascular fitness tests take some time to perform, so the results can be influenced by the attitude of the performer. Scores for the Cooper test, if completed outside, can be affected by the weather, and if subjects work in groups, then group dynamics and attitudes can also affect results.

Harvard step test

The Harvard step test involves the subject stepping on and off a bench, or sturdy box, of 45cm in height (see Figure 5.12). The subject steps fully onto and off the bench for 5 minutes, at a rate of 30 steps per minute. At the end of the exercise, after a 1-minute rest, the subject's pulse rate is counted for 30 seconds. The pulse rate is then doubled (to give a rate per minute). This is often described as a **sub-maximal test** because activity rate is predetermined – the subject does not have to reach a personal maximum rate.

A **fitness rating** is obtained by using the following formula:

$$\frac{100 \times 300 \text{ (length of the exercise in seconds)}}{5.2 \times \text{no. of heart beats per minute}}$$

> This is only a simple formula. Other, more complex formulae can be used, but they require many more readings.

Rating for step test: 90+ = very good; 80+ = good; 65+ = fair; 50+ = poor.

Figure 5.12 Harvard step test

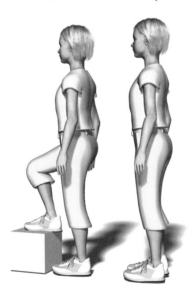

12-minute run test / Cooper test

> Care should be taken with the test protocol. Test results can differ depending on whether the test is done indoors, or outdoors in wind or hot weather.

In the 12-minute run test, or **Cooper test**, the subject runs and / or walks as far as possible in 12 minutes. This is often described as a **maximal test** (i.e. the subject covers as much ground as possible in the time allowed). The fitness level is established by comparing the distance run to established norms for the test.

Ratings for Cooper test (m):

Males: 2600+ = very good; 2400+ = good; 2200+ = fair; 2000+ = poor.
Females: 2200+ = very good; 2000+ = good; 1800+ = fair; 1700+ = poor.

Progressive shuttle-run test

The progressive shuttle-run test is also known as the **bleep test** and the **multi-stage fitness test**. The subject performs continuous shuttle runs between two lines drawn 20 metres apart. The pace is established by a recording that sounds a bleep at the end of each leg of the shuttle run. As the test progresses, the time between the bleeps gets shorter and a level is indicated. When three bleeps in a row are missed, the fitness level of the subject has been established. This is a **maximal test**.

Ratings for this test are given on the recording.

> **The most consistent recordings are on CD because a tape might stretch.**

> **KEY POINT**
>
> Sub-maximal test work is to a specific level. Maximal test work is to the best of your own ability.

Tests for skill related to fitness

AQA	✓
EDEXCEL	✓
OCR	✓
WJEC	✓
CCEA	✓

Agility – The Illinois Agility Run

Agility is a combination of **speed** and **co-ordination**. Both these aspects have to be tested in a protocol that measures agility. The Illinois Agility Run combines a test for running with a test for the ability to change direction around a series of cones following a predetermined pathway (see Figure 5.13).

The subject starts by lying face down behind the start line with their chin on the floor. On the command 'Go', the subject stands up and runs around cones following the prescribed pathway as fast as possible. The measurement is the time taken to complete the run. This can be compared to established norms.

Ratings for Illinois Agility Run (secs):
Males: <15.2 = excellent; <16.1 = good; <18.1 = average; <19.3 = fair; 19.4+ = poor.
Females: <17.0 = excellent; <17.9 = good; <21.7 = average; <23.0 = fair; 23.1+ = poor.

Figure 5.13 Layout of Illinois Agility Run

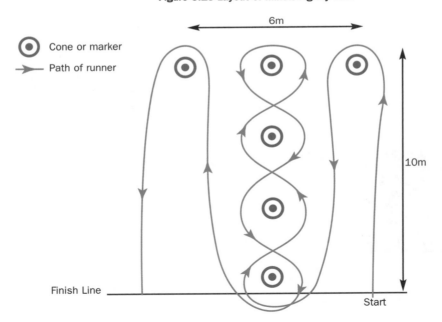

Reaction – The metre-rule drop test

A metre rule is held against a flat wall and the subject stands with their thumb alongside, but **not touching**, the 0cm mark. Without warning, the ruler is dropped and must be caught by gripping between the thumb and index finger (see Figure 5.14). Measurement is the distance between the bottom of the ruler and the index finger.

Ratings for metre-rule drop test (cm):
<8cm = excellent 9–12cm = good; 13–20cm = average; 21+cm = poor

Figure 5.14 Metre-rule drop test

Speed – The timed run

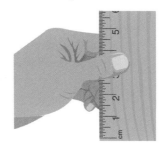

Speed can be tested simply by **timing a run** over an agreed distance, usually less than 100m. Distances are often run in shuttles of around 10m and are usually completed indoors. As the protocol for this test may well vary from place to place, it is not always possible to compare times with established norms. Measurement is taken with a stop watch.

> Shuttle runs include an element of agility (i.e. when the subject turns). This is not included in the timing of straight distance runs. Each type of test is measuring something different.

Balance – The stork stand test

In the **stork stand test**, the subject stands on one foot and places the other foot against the inside of the knee. Hands are placed on hips. Timing starts when both eyes are closed. Timing stops when either the eyes open, the foot parts from the knee or the subject loses their balance (see Figure 5.15).

Figure 5.15 The stork stand test

Co-ordination

AQA	X
EDEXCEL	X
OCR	X
WJEC	✓
CCEA	✓

The alternate-hand wall toss test

In the alternate-hand wall toss test, the subject stands 2m from a wall and tosses a tennis ball under-arm against the wall from one hand and catches it with the other hand. This action is repeated with the throwing and catching being continuous. Measurement is the total number of catches made in 30 seconds.

It is accepted that two or three 'fluke' catches can skew the scores for this test. To avoid this, test protocols permit, but do not insist on, a target area to be put on the wall to aid the accuracy of the throws. They also allow participants to practise the test several times before assessment, suggesting that this might produce more accurate results. However, these permissions call into question the test's objectivity and reliability.

Rating for alternate-hand wall toss test: 35+ = excellent; 30–34 = good; 20–29 = average; 15–19 = fair; <15 = poor.

Body fat composition

AQA	X
EDEXCEL	X
OCR	X
WJEC	X
CCEA	✓

Test for body fat composition

In the test for body fat composition, three skinfold measurements are taken on the body using special callipers. The callipers are designed to measure the thickness of the skin and the fat directly beneath it. Taking these measurements correctly requires some expertise. The results are then totalled and, by using a nomogram (i.e. a graph with more than two scales) collated with age, the percentage of body fat is established.

There are a number of different protocols for this type of testing: some use the Jackson Pollock Equation; others use alternative tables. All the tests rely on spring-loaded callipers, the springs of which can lose their elasticity over time, thereby, giving a suspect reading.

The use of skin callipers **does not** give a true indication of **lean body mass**, and the incorrect use of skin callipers can cause unnecessary distress to some subjects.

BMI

AQA	X
EDEXCEL	X
OCR	✓
WJEC	X
CCEA	X

The **Body-mass Index** (**BMI**) is an estimate of body composition. It is found by using the following formula: BMI = Weight (kg) ÷ Height (m^2)

BMI is often used as an indicator of obesity on the **assumption** that the higher the Index, the greater the level of body fat. However, this assumption is **not always true**. Some well-developed athletes, such as weight-lifters and rugby players (forwards, especially) are very heavy due to their large muscle bulk and this would give a high index. They would be falsely classified as obese.

> **PROGRESS CHECK**
>
> 1. Which tests measure the strength and endurance in the upper arm?
> 2. What is a sub-maximal test?
>
> 2. A test that works to a specific level.
> 1. Pull-ups / chins and dips

Sample GCSE questions

1 (a) What component of physical fitness would you be testing if you used a hand grip dynamometer?

The strength of the hand / lower arm. **(1)**

(b) Give **two** reasons why it is important to follow correct procedures when carrying out fitness tests.

To ensure validity / To ensure safety / To allow comparability. **(2)**

> Any two of these would be satisfactory.

2 (a) Which of the following measure power?

Standing high jump (SHJ)
Sit-and-reach
Standing long jump (SLJ)
Skin callipers

> Make sure you know what the abbreviations stand for.

SHJ and SLJ **(2)**

(b) (i) Name **three** recognised tests of aerobic power.

12-minute run / Cooper run.
Harvard step test.
Bleep test / Multi-stage fitness test. **(3)**

(ii) Describe fully the protocol for the three tests you gave in part (i).

The 12 minute run / Cooper test requires a person to run / walk as far as possible in 12 minutes.

The Harvard step test requires a person to step on and off a 45cm box for 5 minutes at 30 steps / min. The pulse rate is taken after a 1-minute rest.

> Knowledge of protocol distances and scoring systems must be shown.

The Bleep test / Multi-stage fitness test requires a person to complete 20m shuttle runs at the pace of the recording. **(12)**

Exam practice questions

1 What physical component of fitness does the shoulder lift test measure?

.... **(1)**

2 Name one aspect of fitness that can be measured.

.... **(1)**

3 Explain the difference between muscular strength and muscular endurance.

....

....

.... **(4)**

4 **(a)** What does the Harvard step test measure?

.... **(1)**

(b) Explain how the test is administered.

....

....

....

....

.... **(4)**

5 **(a)** Name a test for balance.

.... **(1)**

(b) Describe the protocol for this test.

....

....

....

....

.... **(4)**

6 Factors affecting performance

The following topics are covered in this chapter:

- **The digestive system**
- **Food and diet**
- **Lifestyle, illness and injury**
- **Physical make-up**
- **How personal factors affect performance**
- **Environmental conditions**
- **Drugs used in sport**

6.1 The digestive system

LEARNING SUMMARY	After studying this section you should be able to understand:
	- the functions of the alimentary canal
	- peristalsis

Alimentary canal

AQA	✗
EDEXCEL	✗
OCR	✗
WJEC	✗
CCEA	✓

The main parts of the digestive system are...

- the **mouth**
- the **gullet (oesophagus)**
- the **stomach**
- the **small intestine**
- the **large intestine**
- the **anus**.

These parts form a pathway that food follows through the body. This pathway is called the **alimentary canal** (see Figure 6.1).

Figure 6.1 Alimentary canal

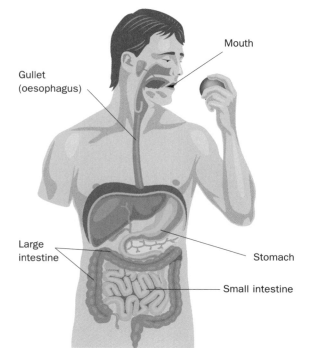

Mouth

Gullet (oesophagus)

Large intestine

Stomach

Small intestine

> You must be able to describe the parts of the alimentary canal.

Each part of the alimentary canal has a separate function (see Table 6.1).

Table 6.1 Functions of the alimentary canal

Mouth	Takes in food and drink, chews and swallows food in small amounts. (A small amount is referred to as a **bolus** of food.)
Oesophagus	Transports the food from the mouth to the stomach by a wave of muscular contraction called peristalsis.
Stomach	Holds food while digestion begins; the absorption of nutrients commences.
Small intestine	Continues with the digestive process and the absorption of nutrients through its approximate length of 6 metres.
Large intestine	Water and some salts are removed at this stage whilst solid waste is stored at the end of the intestine in the bowel.
Anus	This is the end of the alimentary canal through which waste products are excreted from the body.

Make sure you can describe the functions of each part of the alimentary canal.

Peristalsis

When food is transported from the mouth to the stomach it does not just drop into the stomach by force of gravity. It has to be **forced** through the oesophagus. The walls of the oesophagus are made of **smooth muscle** (see page 14), which is laid in long sheaths. These sheaths or long layers of muscle fibre can contract and relax with a **wave-like motion**. This means that the **bolus** (lump) of food can be **pushed** down the oesophagus by the actions of the muscle (see Figure 6.2a). This action is like pushing a marble through a tight rubber tube with your hand (see Figure 6.2b). It is because of this **peristaltic action** that a person standing on their head could still swallow a sandwich or a drink. The forcing of the bolus **upwards** towards the stomach confirms the wave-like muscular movement through the oesophagus.

Figure 6.2a

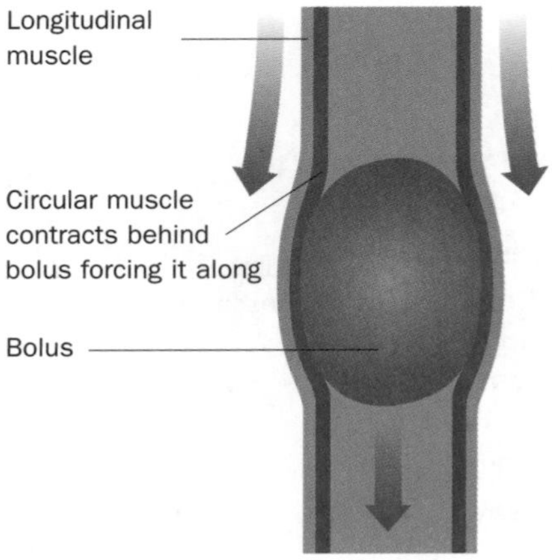

Longitudinal muscle

Circular muscle contracts behind bolus forcing it along

Bolus

Figure 6.2b

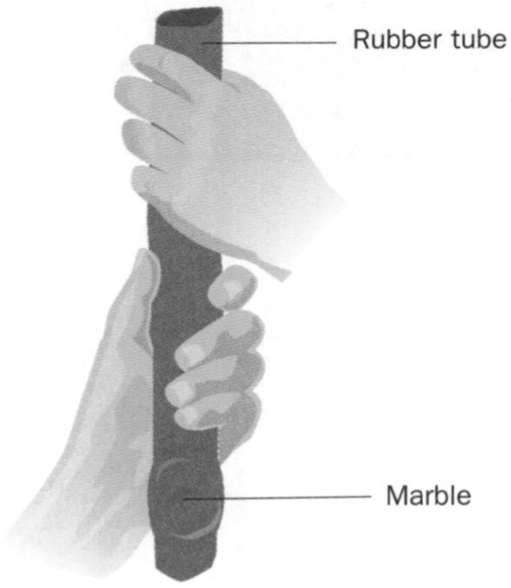

Rubber tube

Marble

PROGRESS CHECK

1. Where does the alimentary canal start and finish?
2. What is a bolus?
3. Where does digestion first begin?
4. Give the correct name for the wave-like motion of the oesophagus.

1. It starts at the mouth, and finishes at the anus. 2. A lump of food. 3. In the stomach. 4. Peristalsis.

6.2 Food and diet

LEARNING SUMMARY

After studying this section you should be able to understand:

- the components of a healthy diet
- the importance of a balanced diet
- the relationship between diet and exercise
- how energy is produced

Healthy diets

AQA	✓
EDEXCEL	✓
OCR	✓
WJEC	✓
CCEA	✓

> You should be able to describe the main foodstuffs needed for a healthy diet.

The essential components of a healthy diet are...

- fruit and vegetables
- cereals and grains
- eggs, cheese, meat and fish
- milk and other milk products.

These food groups provide all the essential **nutrients** for the sports performer (see Figure 6.3).

Figure 6.3 The healthy heptagon

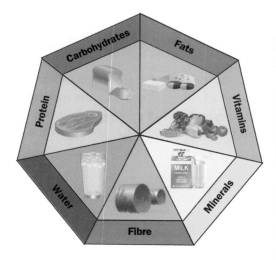

Carbohydrates	These are broken down to glucose to provide fast-release energy. Carbohydrates provide approximately 55% of our energy.
Protein	This provides the 'fabric' for most of the soft tissues. A good protein intake is essential for growth and repair. Proteins provide approximately 15% of our energy.
Water	As most of the body is water we need to constantly replace that which is lost in urine, sweat and breathing, by taking in fluids.
Fats	These contain lots of energy which can be stored for slow-release energy. Fats provide approximately 30% of our energy.
Vitamins	Vitamin A (in milk, butter and fish) contributes to healthy skin and good night vision. Vitamin C (in citrus fruits and vegetables) helps to prevent scurvy. Vitamin D (in milk, fish, eggs and from sunshine) prevents rickets. Only a small amount of these vitamins are needed.
Minerals	Iron from liver and green vegetables prevents thyroid problems. Calcium from milk and cheese produces strong teeth and bones. Only a small amount of minerals is needed.
Fibre	Fibre/roughage is indigestible plant material, which gives the gut something to push on, helping to avoid constipation.

The sources and functions of nutrients are shown in Table 6.2 and Table 6.3.

Table 6.2 Sources of nutrients

> Make sure you can give examples of foodstuffs that contain proteins, carbohydrates, fats, vitamins and minerals.

Nutrient	Source
Proteins	Found in meats, cheese, fish, eggs, soya, nuts.
Carbohydrates	Found in flour foods (breads), sugar foods (jams), dried fruit.
Fats	Found in milk products (butter, cream), lard, nuts, fish, meat.
Vitamins and minerals	Found in the whole range of foodstuffs.

Table 6.3 Functions of nutrients

Nutrient	Function
Proteins	Needed for growth, and the building and repair of body cells.
Carbohydrates	Provide energy.
Fats	Provide energy and insulation, often stored under the skin.
Vitamins	Help in the formation of bodily tissues (hair, teeth, skin, nails) and are necessary for all chemical reactions in the body.
Minerals	Essential for the uptake of vitamins, the formation of bodily tissues and the carrying out of chemical reactions.

You need to know the functions of proteins, carbohydrates, fats, vitamins and minerals.

The bulk of most fruit and vegetables is made up of **fibre**. Fibre is essential to a healthy diet, although it is not a nutrient. It helps to keep the digestion system working. **High-fibre** foods usually provide little energy, but make you feel fuller. This can help in weight loss. (Weight loss should **always** be carefully monitored.)

Non-nutrients are just as essential to a healthy diet as nutrients.

Water is present in many foods and drinks, and is essential to your diet. Like fibre it is not a nutrient, but is needed to replace liquids lost through sweating or passing of urine, and for the chemical reactions that take place in the body.

Balanced diets

> **KEY POINT**
>
> Excess food = Increase in fat; Insufficient food = No energy reserves.

Not all diets are healthy. The food taken in must provide all the nutrients for body growth and the energy for exercise. A balanced diet must contain all the nutrients you need in the correct amount. A varied / balanced diet must have a plentiful supply of fruit and vegetables and must not contain too much fat (see Table 6.4).

Table 6.4 Balanced diets

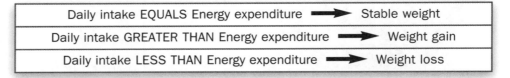

Daily intake EQUALS Energy expenditure ⟶	Stable weight
Daily intake GREATER THAN Energy expenditure ⟶	Weight gain
Daily intake LESS THAN Energy expenditure ⟶	Weight loss

Diet and exercise

Involvement in hard physical exercise does not seem to have any long-term effects on the digestive system. However, during hard physical exercise, blood is diverted from the stomach to the working muscles. This means that any food in the stomach cannot be absorbed during the exercise. Often the body will try to get rid of this food during exercise by vomiting.

> **KEY POINT**
>
> The stomach must not be overloaded before hard work.

Diet is of major importance to the sportsperson. Different performers require different kinds of food, reflecting the different types of physical activity that they undertake. For example, a diet to provide muscle bulk is not the same as a diet to improve stamina.

For example...

- sprinters and weightlifters require lots of **protein** for **muscle bulk**
- long-distance runners require lots of **carbohydrates** for **endurance**.

In addition, a person's diet may well change prior to competition. The aims of the pre-competition diet may be to...

- build up stores of carbohydrates so that energy can be produced for longer periods of time (carbohydrate loading)
- enter the competition with as little in the stomach as possible – this helps the breathing process
- prevent gastric disturbances – the competitor should avoid gas-making foods, such as onions, baked beans and cabbage
- provide a positive psychological attitude – if a good diet is followed, it will provide a sense of well-being before and during competition (see Figure 6.4).

Figure 6.4 Ways to achieve carbohydrate loading

Days before competition: 7	6	5	4	3	2	1		Approx. rise in muscle glycogen
normal training diet and activity							competition day	normal
hard session		low carbohydrate diet		high carbohydrate diet				140% increase
		hard session		high carbohydrate diet				90% increase
				high carbohydrate diet				50% increase

- **During** physical activity, foodstuffs should be avoided, but performers should drink liquids – especially water – to replace losses brought about by sweating and energy production, and to help maintain body temperature.
- **After** hard physical activity, it is important to continue replacing lost fluid, and eating food replaces depleted energy stores. But eating should be delayed for one to two hours after competition. If a meal is taken directly after activity, blood is directed to the stomach from the muscles, where it is still assisting in the recovery process (i.e. the removal of lactic acid).

KEY POINT

Post-competition diet should not be overlooked. It should include early replacement of liquid to compensate for fluid loss, followed later by ingestion of carbohydrates to help replace energy stores.

Energy production

In order to walk or run, our muscles must be able to contract. To do this they need energy. Muscles get most of their energy when **glucose** and **oxygen** react together. Oxygen is obtained by normal breathing; glucose comes from the food we eat.

You must know this simple process.

Foods such as bread, potatoes and rice contain **carbohydrate**.
Carbohydrate is digested to form **glucose**.
Glucose passes through the wall of the stomach into the **blood**.
The blood carries some glucose to the **muscles**.
The glucose is stored in the muscles as **glycogen**.
The glycogen breaks down to glucose when the muscles work to produce **energy**.

Remember the glycogen storage areas.

The blood also carries some glucose to be stored as glycogen in the **liver**. From here it can be released to the muscles via the blood, when needed.

Muscles obtain energy for contraction from the breakdown of **ATP** into **ADP**. It is this process or **glycolysis** (i.e. the breakdown of glucose) that produces enough energy to rebuild ATP from ADP, so that muscle contraction can continue. Oxygen and glucose react together to produce energy in the form of ATP. If a large and continuous supply of oxygen is available, then the energy is produced by the **aerobic system**.

> **KEY POINT**
>
> Aerobic respiration: Glucose + Oxygen = Energy + Two waste products (Water and Carbon dioxide)

The waste products that are excreted are...
- water in urine and sweat
- carbon dioxide, by breathing out.

During very hard physical exercise, there is not enough oxygen for the aerobic system to produce energy. When this happens the **anaerobic system** is used.

> **KEY POINT**
>
> Anaerobic respiration: Glucose = Small amount of energy quickly + Waste product (Lactic acid)

Lactic acid can only be removed when it combines with oxygen. As there is not enough oxygen, lactic acid builds up, eventually forcing the muscles to stop working. This is described as an oxygen debt (O_2 debt). The only way to get rid of this oxygen debt is to stop working and breathe in large amounts of oxygen. When the debt has been repaid, then physical work can begin again (see page 39).

> **PROGRESS CHECK**
>
> 1. Name the seven components of the healthy heptagon.
> 2. For what purpose does the body use carbohydrates?
> 3. Explain the disadvantages of eating a meal just prior to a competition.
>
> 3. During competition, blood is diverted from the stomach to the working muscles, therefore food cannot be absorbed. It can lead to under-performance and / or vomiting.
> 2. To provide energy.
> 1. Carbohydrates; Fats; Vitamins; Minerals; Fibre; Water; Protein.

6.3 Lifestyle, illness and injury

LEARNING SUMMARY

After studying this section you should be able to understand:
- how lifestyle might affect performance
- how illness and injuries affect performance

Lifestyle

AQA ✓
EDEXCEL ✓
OCR ✓
WJEC ✓
CCEA ✓

Training for fitness not only includes the correct physical work, but also means living in a healthy way. It is not possible to 'burn the candle at both ends' and still produce a good class of performance. People take part in exercise in order to...

- promote and improve health and fitness
- obtain **social**, **mental** and **physical benefits**.

Figure 6.5 Benefits triangle

Social
Benefits

Health and Fitness

Physical
Benefits

Mental
Benefits

KEY POINT

The most suitable lifestyle for an athlete is a healthy lifestyle. This includes physical, mental and social well-being.

- **Physical well-being** refers to a person's physical fitness – a body that works well, and is free from illness and injury.
- **Mental well-being** refers to a relaxed attitude – a mind that is free from stress and worry.
- **Social well-being** refers to a warm, contented, well-fed existence in a settled social setting.

Remember these points by using the mnemonic 'SLASHED'.

To live a healthy lifestyle you must consider all of the following:

SL – sleep – an essential part of any training programme, sleep needs to be ample and of good quality.

A – attitude – a positive attitude is essential in the sportsperson. Attitude includes having **respect** for opponents and fellow players. Like approach to competition, respect for others is essential and it can help, indirectly, to produce a better individual performance.

S – smoking – smoking tobacco makes you smell, can ruin your health and may eventually kill you. Avoid it!

Make sure you can describe the 'SLASHED' approach to life.

H – hygiene – good personal hygiene helps you to avoid infection and makes you feel good. For the athlete, good foot care is essential. Athlete's foot and verrucae can be avoided by wearing clean, suitable, disinfected footwear.

E – environment – living in a pollution-free situation can help to avoid respiratory illnesses. Also, climate and the weather can affect performance. Living at high altitude, where the air is thinner and oxygen levels are lower, can enhance performance in anaerobic activities such as power events.

D – diet – the correct balanced diet can help you to cope with the everyday stresses of life.

There are a number of indicators that an individual may notice, which might reflect their state of well-being. An overall positive attitude towards, and a satisfaction with, life in general are good indications of well-being. These are often supported by a desire to participate in activities either alone or with others.

Illness and injury

AQA	✓
EDEXCEL	✓
OCR	✓
WJEC	✓
CCEA	✓

Being fit does not prevent **illness**, although a fit person should recover from both illness and injury more quickly than an unfit person. **Injury** is one of the biggest problems that can face a sportsperson; it is often the single most limiting factor relating to performance. Prevention is better than cure, and injuries are best avoided by…

- **training** correctly and with the aim of developing those factors that are important for the event
- doing sufficient **warm-up activities**, including flexibility and stretching exercises to help prepare the body for work, and warming down
- using **protective equipment**, such as mouth guards, shin pads and helmets that are designed to protect the player as well as enhance performance
- wearing the **correct clothing** for the sport concerned; for example, ill-fitting shorts can chafe the inside of the leg and poorly fitting footwear can lead to a host of leg and foot injuries
- playing to the **rules of the sport** – rules are not just about fair play, but were devised with safety in mind – referees and umpires are duty-bound to enforce the rules to help protect the players
- checking that the **environment is safe**.

Injuries caused by violence are common in both contact and non-contact sports. Most sports injuries occur during contact with…

- **an opponent**, e.g. during a tackle in soccer
- **an implement**, e.g. striking a volley ball incorrectly can cause finger injuries
- **the playing surface**, e.g. playing rugby on frozen ground.

The identification of injuries is considered more closely in Chapter 7 (see pages 96–100).

Figure 6.6 Protective clothing for hockey goalkeeper

Make sure you know the main causes of injury.

PROGRESS CHECK

1. List the three main states of well-being.
2. What does SLASHED stand for?
3. List four pieces of protective clothing found in sport, and name the sports they are used in.

3. **Any suitable answers, e.g.** Gum shield – rugby; Shin pads – football; Helmet – cycling; Kickers – hockey.
2. Sleep; Attitude; Smoking; Hygiene; Environment; Diet.
1. Physical; Mental; Social.

6.4 Physical make-up

LEARNING SUMMARY

After studying this section you should be able to understand:

- how a person's physical make-up is described
- how physical make-up influences performance

Describing physical make-up

AQA	✓
EDEXCEL	✓
OCR	✓
WJEC	✓
CCEA	✓

Successful competitors in different sports tend to have different body types. Whilst it is true that not all basketball players are over two metres tall, there is no denying the fact that height is important in basketball. It is also true that most sumo wrestlers have a very heavy physique and that female gymnasts tend to be of short stature.

> Learn what the word 'somatotype' means and be able to describe the three main traits.

The classification of body types is called **somatotyping** and was first introduced by an American called William Sheldon. Sheldon established that there were three main traits in all body types: **endomorph**, **mesomorph** and **ectomorph**. As all people have some of each trait present in their build, each person is measured for each trait on a scale of 1–7.

- A person rating 7 as an endomorph has a large amount of body fat.
- A person rating 7 as a mesomorph is broad-shouldered and muscular.
- A person rating 7 as an ectomorph is tall and thin.

Figure 6.7 Three examples of extreme somatotypes

Table 6.5 Features of the three somatotypes

Mesomorph	Ectomorph	Endomorph
Very muscular	Very thin	Very fat
Large head	Narrow face, high forehead	Fatty upper arms
Broad shoulders	Narrow shoulders	Narrow shoulders
Strong forearms	Thin, narrow chest	Relatively thin wrists
Strong thighs	Thin, narrow abdomen	Fatty thighs
Narrow hips	Slim hips	Wide hips

Physical make-up and performance

The average somatotype rating would be 4.4.4 (i.e. a bit of everything), but this is rarely found. Top level sports players tend to show extremes of one or other of the scales. These can be shown by using a **somatotype triangle** (see Figure 6.8).

Figure 6.8 Somatotype triangle

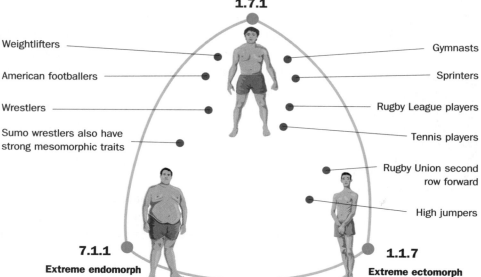

Extreme mesomorph
1.7.1

Weightlifters

American footballers

Wrestlers

Sumo wrestlers also have strong mesomorphic traits

Gymnasts

Sprinters

Rugby League players

Tennis players

Rugby Union second row forward

High jumpers

7.1.1
Extreme endomorph

1.1.7
Extreme ectomorph

> You should be able to give examples of sporting activities related to each of the three body types.

While both men and women can be included in somatotyping, it must be remembered that the body shape and size of boys and girls changes as they get older (see page 85).

PROGRESS CHECK

1. Describe the body somatotype that a successful weightlifter might have.
2. In a somatotype rating, which body type does each number refer to?
3. What sport would an extreme endomorph be best suited to?

1. Mesomorph (i.e. broad shoulders and very muscular).
2. First number = endomorph; Second number = mesomorph; Third number = ectomorph.
3. E.g. Sumo wrestling.

6.5 How personal factors affect performance

LEARNING SUMMARY

After studying this section you should be able to understand:

- how a person's history and status might affect their performance
- the effect that age might have on performance
- some of the effects of gender on performance
- how a person's approach might affect their performance

Factors affecting performance

AQA ✓
EDEXCEL ✓
OCR ✓
WJEC ✓
CCEA ✓

History and status

Before embarking on any sort of training programme, it is essential that the background of the sportsperson is studied. Factors that can influence the amount of physical work a person may be able to do are outlined below:

- **Medical history** – has the person suffered serious injury or illness in the past? Do they have a physical disability to be considered?
- **Medical status** – is the person suffering from any illness at this time? (Asthmatics and diabetics can and do carry out a great deal of physical activity, but their coaches should be aware of their condition).
- **Weight** – is the person a suitable weight for their age and, if not, is there a reason for this?
- **Experience** – how experienced is the performer? (This might determine the level of performance. For example, an inexperienced judo player could be in danger if he were to fight an experienced opponent).

Make sure you can describe the relevant background information about a person that needs to be considered before they can start a fitness programme.

Age and performance

Age affects performance in a number of ways:

- **Strength** – full strength is often not attained until a person is in their early 20s, and muscular strength can be improved throughout their 30s.
- **Injury** – older people are more prone to injury than young people. They often take longer to recover from injury.
- **Flexibility** – the very young are very flexible, and this continues with women into their teens. By their 30s, men in particular tend to have lost much of their flexibility.
- **Reaction time** – this tends to slow down with age.
- **Experience** – older people tend to make up for their reduced physical capabilities by using their skill levels to better effect. This is known as experience.
- **Stamina** – this is often a feature of the older performer. Sprint speed may have reduced with age, but endurance often increases.

Figure 6.9 Influence of age on performance

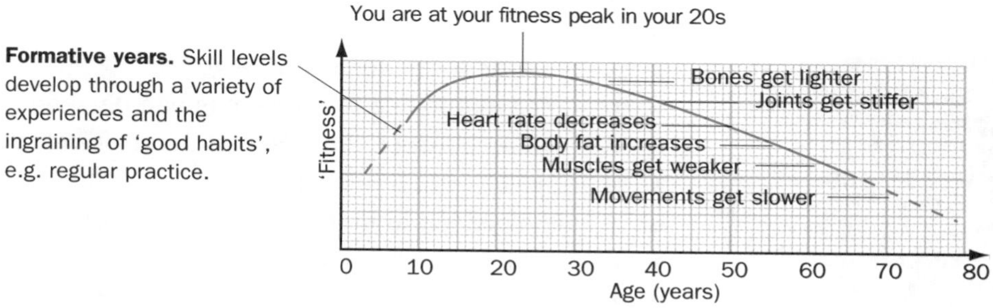

Formative years. Skill levels develop through a variety of experiences and the ingraining of 'good habits', e.g. regular practice.

You are at your fitness peak in your 20s

Bones get lighter
Joints get stiffer
Heart rate decreases
Body fat increases
Muscles get weaker
Movements get slower

'Fitness'

0   10   20   30   40   50   60   70   80
Age (years)

Gender

Up to the age of approximately 10 years, boys and girls are very similar in size and build. However, once puberty is reached, significant changes can be observed in both sexes.

During male puberty...

- **testosterone** makes boys bigger and stronger
- strength-to-weight ratio increases
- **bigger** muscles and bones develop
- **weight** increases
- the heart and lungs become bigger.

During female puberty...

- the **pelvis** often becomes wider to aid in future childbirth
- **flexibility** is more pronounced
- a higher percentage of body fat is maintained
- the onset of **menstruation** can affect body weight, size and, therefore, performance.

Figure 6.10 Influence of menstrual cycle on performance

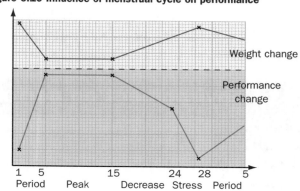

Weight change

Performance change

1   5   15   24   28   5
Period   Peak   Decrease Stress Period

Approach

A positive, logical approach is essential if the highest levels of performance are to be attained. To assist in this approach the performer should set targets to aim for. These targets or goals help to show progress, show how effective planning is and help to increase self confidence.

Goal setting is the process of devising attainable targets that often help in the training process. These targets or goals are designed to lead to an ultimate long-term goal, such as winning an event at the Olympics. Long-term goals are broken down into medium-term and short-term goals, where the performer can see success as being easily attainable. These goals are like small stepping stones to the ultimate long-term goal.

Goal-setting helps in training because success builds up confidence and helps to increase motivation (see page 60). There is a 'SMARTER' or 'SMART' way to remember how effective short-term and medium-term goals should be. These goals should be...

- S – specific to the long-term target
- M – measurable, so that progress can be seen
- A – agreed between the coach and the individual
- R – realistic, i.e. attainable
- T – time-phased to fit into the long-term goal
- E – exciting, just like the ultimate goal
- R – recorded so that progress can be seen.

'SMARTER' is the mnemonic used by some exam boards. Other exam boards use 'SMART', where A stands for 'Agreed and Achievable', and R stands for 'Realistic and Recordable'.

Each goal should be a target to aim for.

PROGRESS CHECK

1. What is the difference between medical history and medical status?
2. What effect does age have on reaction time?
3. What is the major effect of testosterone on boys?

1. Medical history relates to past injuries and illnesses. Medical status relates to ongoing illnesses, e.g. asthma, diabetes.
2. Age slows down reaction time.
3. It makes boys bigger and stronger.

6.6 Environmental conditions

LEARNING SUMMARY	After studying this section you should be able to understand:
	• the effects that environment might have on performance

Effect of environment on performance

AQA ✓
EDEXCEL ✓
OCR ✓
WJEC ✓
CCEA ✓

KEY POINT

Training should acclimatise the individual for known competitive conditions.

The main environmental factors to be considered are:

- **Weather** – it can be too hot, cold, humid or windy for a person to produce a high-level performance. Few athletes can produce their best performances when it is raining or very cold. The training programme should **reflect** the anticipated conditions that will prevail when the competition is due to take place. Remember, it is not just the cold that can affect performance. How many 'fun runners' train in the evenings after work for a half marathon and then find that the event takes place in the heat of the day?

- **Pollution** – this has become more and more a factor in the performance of sporting events. Pollution can have a considerable effect on sporting events, especially **endurance events** that use the aerobic system. Asthmatics and others with breathing problems could be disadvantaged. Pollution was anticipated to be one of the major concerns for the 2008 Beijing Olympics.

- **State of the sports arena** – the track or the sports field can influence performance. Pitches with long or wet grass will slow players down. Long grass can also affect the movement of a ball in a game. **Artificial surfaces** will affect performance if a player is used to grass. Inside, **a dusty or wet floor** in a gymnasium can be slippery and is, therefore, very dangerous.

- **Venue** – the training programme should take into account where the event will be held. This is especially so if the event is to take place at **altitude**. The Mexico Games in 1968 took place 7350 feet (2240m) above sea level. At this level the air is 25% thinner than at sea level. An athlete's ability to take in and absorb oxygen would be much impaired without prior altitude training.

> You must know the effects and problems of competing at high altitude.

PROGRESS CHECK

1. How could long grass affect performance in soccer?
2. Explain why altitude can affect physical performance.

2. The air is thinner so performers have difficulty absorbing oxygen.
1. The ball will roll more slowly, a player will run more slowly, and the player will find it difficult to turn quickly.

6.7 Drugs used in sport

LEARNING SUMMARY

After studying this section you should be able to understand:
- which drugs are used in sport
- the control of drugs in sport

Drugs used in sport

AQA	✓
EDEXCEL	✓
OCR	✓
WJEC	✓
CCEA	✓

Drugs in sport are regarded as **ergogenic aids** – substances that enhance performance.

The use of some drugs is quite acceptable in sport: people who suffer from asthma or hay fever, for example, are allowed to take suitably approved drugs. The use of some prescribed drugs to overcome illness is also acceptable. What is considered unacceptable is the **abuse** or **misuse** of drugs in order to enhance performance.

> **KEY POINT**
>
> There are many different types of drugs used in sport. Some are **used** and some are **abused**.

> You must have a sound knowledge of the banned groups of drugs and how they can enhance performance.

Drug	Description	
Stimulants	**Increase alertness** and **reduce fatigue**. They can increase competitiveness and aggression. They can also cause depression.	
Alcohol	Can induce **feelings of well-being** and **lack of responsibility**. It can lead to aggression, reduced glycogen levels, and kidney and liver damage.	
Tobacco	A **relaxant** but it **reduces oxygen-carrying capabilities**. It **increases heart rate and blood pressure** and can lead to blocked arteries, excessive coughing, emphysema and possibly cancer.	
Blood doping	This is a **forbidden practice** rather than a drug. After training, an athlete removes red cells from their blood, freezes them and re-injects them prior to competition. This gives a **high red cell count** that improves the carrying of oxygen to the muscles, which is necessary for long-distance runners. This can damage the liver and kidneys. The development of **EPO** (erythropoietin) in the 1990s, a drug that artificially stimulates the production of excessive red cells, has similar effects.	
Anabolic agents (steroids)	These **accelerate** the **growth and repair** of **muscle** and are often abused to help 'bulk up' for explosive events. This can cause heart and blood pressure problems, excess aggression, male characteristics in females and possible loss of fertility.	
Peptide hormones, mimetics and analogues	These have similar effects to steroids. Many are **artificially produced**.	
Beta-blockers	These are taken to help the performer **relax** and counteract the effects of adrenaline. Often used in archery and shooting, they can cause **abnormal blood pressure**, **insomnia**, and **depression**.	

Drug	Description	
Diuretics	**Remove fluids** by excessive urination to bring about speedy **short-term weight loss**. These are often useful for boxers and wrestlers who have to make a certain weight category. Diuretics cause the loss of soluble vitamins and minerals and can act as **masking agents** for other banned substances.	
Narcotic analgesics (painkillers)	These are used to suppress pain from injury and can **increase the pain threshold** during competition. This can lead to the injuries worsening. Examples are heroin, morphine and codeine.	

Many people see the use of these banned drugs as a form of **cheating** because they enhance performance. This is seen as being **morally wrong**. However, these drugs are also banned because of the **dangerous side effects** that they can have on the people who take them.

> **KEY POINT**
>
> Many drugs are banned in order to protect the performer.

Control of drug abuse

Not all drugs are banned by the **International Olympic Committee** (IOC), but in 1998 a massive scandal relating to drug abuse in cycling was exposed. Following the scandal, the IOC, with the support of a number of countries, set up the **World Anti-Doping Agency**. The ultimate goal of **WADA** is for all athletes to benefit from the same anti-doping procedures, regardless of the sport or the country where testing might take place. This is seen as the best way to produce a 'level playing field' for all performers.

However, whilst WADA can recommend the **best codes of practice** for the implementation of testing for drug abuse both in-competition and out-of-competition, its authority relies on the support of participating countries and sports.

WADA publishes a **Prohibited List** of banned substances and methods, which it updates and revises continually each year. Individual countries and sports perform drug testing and decide on their own levels of punishment. This allows for some variance in the interpretation of the Prohibited List and the level of punishment by the different countries and sports.

> **PROGRESS CHECK**
>
> 1. What are drugs in sport also known as?
> 2. What types of drugs are permitted in sport?
> 3. What effect do beta-blockers have, and which sports might they be used in?
> 4. **(a)** What does EPO stand for? **(b)** What does WADA stand for?
>
> 4. **(a)** Erythropoietin. **(b)** World Anti-Doping Agency.
> 3. They help in relaxation and counteract the effects of adrenaline. They could be used in archery and shooting.
> 2. Treatments for asthma, hay fever, etc.
> 1. Ergogenic aids.

Sample GCSE questions

1 Where is the oesophagus?

Between the mouth and the stomach. **(1)**

2 Body type is a factor that can determine potential performance in sport. What are the three scales used to establish somatotype?

Endomorph, Mesomorph, Ectomorph. **(3)**◀ Overall shape, hip size and shoulder size are the important features in each of these scales.

3 **(a)** Describe the characteristics of an extreme ectomorph.

Linear in shape, thin, narrow shoulders and hips, has little muscle or fat. **(4)**

   (b) Select a sport or event in which those with ectomorphic tendencies may excel.

High jump; Long-distance running; Basketball. **(1)**◀ Any one of these answers would be suitable.

4 What effect does age have on flexibility for men?

Flexibility is reduced as men get older. **(1)**◀ Be aware of the range of effects of ageing on both men and women.

5 **(a)** State **two** physical dangers that athletes may face if they take anabolic steroids.

Kidney / liver damage; Male characteristics in females; Heart disease; Cancer; High blood pressure; Infertility. **(2)**◀ The question clearly asks for two physical dangers. Any two of these answers would be suitable – not all of them.

   (b) State **two** reasons why an athlete might take anabolic steroids despite the risks.

To increase training potential; To win; To gain wealth; To increase aggression; To improve power; To improve strength; To enhance performance. **(2)**◀ There is a wide range of possible answers but the question only asks for two, so choose only two.

Exam practice questions

1   List the four food groups that do not provide energy.

....

....

.... **(4)**

2   Which food groups would provide the main source of energy for the following events?

(a)   100-metre sprint ....

(b)   5 minutes of jogging ....

(c)   3 hours of cycling ....

(d)   Running a marathon .... **(4)**

3   Which body somatotype would be best suited to the following activities?

(a)   100-metre sprint ....

(b)   High jump ....

(c)   Boxing ....

(d)   Rowing .... **(4)**

4   Explain the term WADA. What is its ultimate goal?

....

....

.... **(4)**

7 Safety in sport

The following topics are covered in this chapter:

- **Safe practice**
- **Health and hygiene**
- **Types of injuries**
- **Sports injuries**
- **Specific sports injuries**

7.1 Safe practice

LEARNING SUMMARY	After studying this section you should be able to understand:
	- how to participate safely in sport
	- the Health and Safety at Work Act, with regard to sport

Acting safely

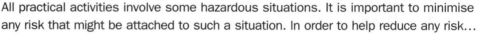

AQA	✓
EDEXCEL	✓
OCR	✓
WJEC	✓
CCEA	✓

All practical activities involve some hazardous situations. It is important to minimise any risk that might be attached to such a situation. In order to help reduce any risk...

- check to see that all **equipment** is in good working order
- check to ensure that the **playing surface** is in good working order
- always use the correct **playing technique** and follow the **rules**
- consult the person in charge if in doubt about a safety issue.

All organisers should carry out a **Risk Assessment** before starting work. Each different sporting activity requires that certain aspects be considered.

For example, in **gymnastics, trampoline and dance**, the following elements must be considered:

- The condition of mats and floors.
- The presence of **qualified staff** and **spotters**, as appropriate.
- Sufficient head space.
- Observance of the 'no jewellery' rule.
- The wearing of the correct **clothing**, **hand guards** and soft chalk (magnesium carbonate), as appropriate.
- The use of help and the correct method when lifting equipment.

In **games activities**, the following conditions must be ensured:

- The surface is clear of obstructions and debris.
- The surroundings provide a safe area.
- Individual **protective equipment** is always available (e.g. gum shields, face masks, shin pads).
- Group equipment is available and in good condition (e.g. pads, padded gloves).
- Posts are protected and nets properly secured.

In **athletic activities**, the following aspects must be checked:

- Running areas are clear of obstructions and debris.
- Landing areas are clear, with sand well raked and rakes kept clear.
- Throwing areas are well marked-out and caged.
- **Warning sounds** are used to indicate throws taking place.
- No running to collect javelins is allowed.
- Waiting participants stay behind throwers.

In **swimming**, the following precautions must be taken:

- Walking at all times when out of the pool.
- Checking to see where the deep end is.
- Using boards only as directed.
- Jumping or diving only under supervision in a designated area.
- Using only approved **artificial aids**.

In outdoor pursuits, the following safety measures must be carried out:

- The **weather forecast** is checked.
- **Personal equipment and safety / first aid** equipment is checked.
- Appropriate **emergency rations** are available.
- **Detailed routes** and **escape routes** are planned and recorded.
- Copies of plans are left with responsible people together with an expected time of completion.

General considerations relevant to many different sports and activities include...

- following the rules of the National Governing Bodies (NGB)
- being aware of potential risks, and not taking unnecessary risks
- being responsible for your own safety as well as that of others
- following the instructions given.

Lifting and carrying

AQA	✓
EDEXCEL	✗
OCR	✓
WJEC	✗
CCEA	✗

Injuries, sometimes quite serious ones, do occur when equipment is being prepared for an activity.

When **lifting** equipment on your own, you should always...

- bend your knees and keep your arms bent
- keep the load close to your body
- keep a straight back
- lift using the large muscles of your legs
- keep your head up and do not lift above your head without assistance.

When **lowering** equipment, the opposite procedure should be followed – with an emphasis on a straight back.

> **KEY POINT**
>
> The opening and closing of trampoline 'wings' is a job for two people. Although wings are hinged, care should be taken in lifting and lowering, and nothing should be trapped inside them.

When **carrying** equipment, remember that...

- large objects will need at least two people
- multiple carriers must work together, and not pull or push each other
- heads must be kept up so a clear line of sight exists
- work should be matched to the capabilities of the lifters.

Javelins must be carried **vertically**. Javelins can kill, either by being thrown at someone or by someone running onto the end of one.

The 1974 Health and Safety at Work Act

AQA	✓
EDEXCEL	✗
OCR	✗
WJEC	✗
CCEA	✗

Make sure you know the seven main features of the 1974 Health and Safety Act.

Schools, sports / leisure centres and stadia have a **duty of care** to the sports performer. The 1974 Health and Safety Act states that whoever puts on a sporting activity must put the **safety of the performer first and foremost**. They must ensure that...

- all equipment is safe to use
- the group size is appropriate to the activity
- the ability of the group matches the event
- activities and training sessions are properly planned and controlled
- safety equipment is available and in good working order
- first aid is available
- procedures for calling the emergency services are in place.

PROGRESS CHECK

1. What should always be worn while playing sport?
2. What should never be worn while playing sport?
3. What two pieces of information must be included in a planned route?
4. How should javelins be carried?

1. The correct clothes for the sport in question. 2. Jewellery, watches and especially earrings. 3. Escape routes and expected time of completion. 4. Vertically.

7.2 Health and hygiene

LEARNING SUMMARY

After studying this section you should be able to understand:

- what health is
- the problems associated with personal hygiene
- the influence of weight on a healthy body

Health

AQA	✓
EDEXCEL	✓
OCR	✓
WJEC	✓
CCEA	✓

Health is a state of mental, physical and social well-being. It is defined by the **World Health Organisation (WHO)** as a state of complete physical, mental and social well-being, not simply the absence of disease and infirmity.

- **Physical well-being** – all the body systems should be in good working order, with no illness or injury.
- **Mental well-being** – people should have a stress-free attitude, with emotions under control and a 'feel good' frame of mind.
- **Social well-being** – people should have an awareness of their role in society, the support of friends and colleagues and a lifestyle that includes the basic necessities of life (i.e. food, clothing and shelter).
- **Health** is closely associated with diet (see page 77), physical fitness (see page 28) and hygiene (see next page).

Particular attention should be given to **body weight**, as this is often the first indicator of wellness, the condition that minimises the chances of becoming ill. **Weight control**, or **weight management**, is the ability to control body weight by balancing food intake with energy expenditure (see page 78). Having weight in excess of normal (i.e. being overweight), especially if there is a large amount of body fat, can lead to heart and other health problems. Being **underweight** means weighing less than is normal, and this can reduce the body's ability to fight illness and infections.

Obesity is the condition of being severely overweight, where body fat is **above 20%** of total body weight. It places particular strain on the **cardio-vascular** and **cardio-respiratory** systems and can lead to heart disease, high blood pressure, hypertension, diabetes and liver problems. In addition, strain on the skeletal system can lead to chronic backache and damage to the joints (arthritic conditions).

Anorexia, more correctly called **anorexia nervosa**, is a potentially fatal illness. It is the lack of desire to eat, and brings about an extreme low body weight and a distorted body image. It often occurs in female gymnasts and dancers who are under pressure to maintain a low body weight to high-strength ratio. Anorexia sufferers can become very **malnourished**. The condition can also lead to a number of other problems including hair loss, infertility and osteoporosis. As anorexia can be as much a **psychological** as a **physical** problem, it is best treated under medical supervision.

Personal hygiene

Hygiene means making sure that a person is clean, healthy and has good personal habits. This will not stop a person from becoming injured or ill, but will help to prevent some illnesses and aid in the recovery process.

The following are some aspects to consider:
- **Clothing** should be washed regularly, kept clean and should be appropriate to the activity. Clean clothes smell better and help to prevent the spread of bacteria.
- **Teeth** should not only be kept clean, but should be protected by the use of gum shields where necessary.
- **Nails** should be kept clean and short to prevent accidental scratching.
- **Hair** should be kept clean and tidy; long hair should be tied back whilst playing sport.
- **Tissues** and handkerchiefs should be used correctly. Handkerchiefs must be washed regularly and tissues disposed of correctly. These should be used to help prevent the spread of infection when sneezing.
- **Vaccinations** should be used to help stop the spread of diseases: prevention is better than cure. For some sports, such as horse-riding, it is as well to have tetanus injections before starting to ride, not just after an injury.
- **Sweating** produces an excellent breeding ground for bacteria. The use of deodorants only hides the smell of body odour; it does not remove it. Only a good shower can remove body odour.
- **Feet** are of particular concern. Not only should shoes be a good fit to help prevent corns, blisters and bunions, but the feet themselves should be checked on a regular basis for athlete's foot and verrucae. These infections often spread in warm, wet environments such as shower areas. Both are highly contagious.

7.3 Types of injuries

LEARNING SUMMARY

After studying this section you should be able to understand:

- the difference between open and closed soft tissue injuries
- hard tissue injuries

KEY POINT

Medical treatment should be carried out only by a qualified medical practitioner.

Hard and soft tissue injuries

AQA	✓
EDEXCEL	✓
OCR	✗
WJEC	✗
CCEA	✗

Soft tissue injuries

Soft tissue injuries refer to injuries to any part of the body, except bone. They account for over 90% of all sports injuries.

There are two main types of soft tissue injuries: **open wounds** and **closed wounds**.

KEY POINT

Open wounds are those that allow blood to escape (see Table 7.1).

Table 7.1 Open wounds

Type of open wound	Causes
Cuts and grazes	Contact with hard objects and surfaces
Blisters	Repeated rubbing of skin
Chafing	Ill-fitting clothing

Blister

Make sure you know the difference between open and closed wounds.

KEY POINT

Closed wounds are those where there is no external bleeding (see Table 7.2).

Table 7.2 Closed wounds

Type of closed wound	Causes	Symptoms
Bruising	Impact with hard object	Pain, swelling, discolouration
Strained muscle	Stretching of 'cold' muscles	Pain, tenderness
Torn muscle	Poor warm-up, over-stretching, sudden movement	Sharp pain, discolouration
Tendonitis	Repeated stress of tendon	Pain, swelling, inflammation
Sprained ligament	Sudden forcing of joint beyond normal range	Pain, swelling, loss of movement
Meniscal tears*	Violent impact, sudden twisting	Pain, loss of movement

*Meniscal cartilage is wedge-shaped and found in mobile joints such as the knee (see Chapter 1).

Bruising is caused by bleeding under the skin.

Hard tissue injuries

Hard tissue injuries are injuries to **bone tissue** and, fortunately for the sportsperson, they occur far less frequently than soft tissue injuries. Hard tissue injuries are most common in contact sports and are usually caused by contact with…

- an **opponent**, e.g. in a tackle
- an **implement**, e.g. when a hard ball hits the hand
- the **playing surface**, e.g. when falling on frozen ground.

You must know the difference between hard and soft tissue injuries.

A hard tissue injury is called a **fracture** and there are four main types:

1 Closed fracture
2 Open fracture
3 Compound fracture
4 Stress fracture

Both closed and open fractures may be complicated by injury to blood vessels, nerves or adjacent organs caused by fractured bone ends or fragments of bone.

A **closed fracture** is when the bone is broken but the skin is not. An **open fracture** is when the end of the broken bone appears through the surface of the skin. A **compound fracture** is when the broken bone has caused another injury.

The following are the general symptoms of closed fractures, open fractures and compound fractures:

- The break of the bone may be felt or heard.
- Pain and tenderness.
- Swelling and a possible abnormal shape in the painful area.

Figure 7.1 Types of fracture

Closed fracture

Open fracture

Open wound

Stress fractures are cracks that appear along the length of a bone and are caused by repeated stress applied to the bone over a long period of time. In long-distance runners, these are often called **shin soreness** or **shin splints**. The accepted treatment is to stop exercise and seek medical advice.

> **KEY POINT**
>
> Treatment should always be provided by a medical expert.

> **PROGRESS CHECK**
>
> 1 What are the three most common causes of a fracture?
> 2 Explain the term 'compound fracture'.
>
> 1. Contact with an opponent, an implement or hard / frozen ground.
> 2. This is when a broken bone has caused other injuries.

7.4 Sports injuries

LEARNING SUMMARY	After studying this section you should be able to understand:
	● a range of common conditions that might affect the sportsperson

Overuse at joints

AQA	✓
EDEXCEL	✓
OCR	✓
WJEC	✓
CCEA	X

The repeated use of joints can cause specific injuries or conditions, or aggravate existing conditions. For example...

● **inflammation** – this is observed as redness, heat, swelling and pain around the joint
● **arthritis** – this is a collective term for a number of conditions that result in inflammation of a joint
● **osteoarthritis** – this is a specific form of arthritis caused by the wearing away of articular cartilage.

Sufferers of any of these conditions should avoid repeated impact on the affected joints, for example, jumping on hard surfaces. Activities that place less stress on the joints, such as cycling and swimming, are more appropriate.

Osteoporosis

Osteoporosis refers to a group of diseases typified by the reduction of bone mass. Bones tend to become brittle and inclined to fracture. Osteoporosis is often linked to age, lack of exercise or a shortage of calcium and vitamin D in the diet. Regular participation in weight-bearing activities, such as walking, running and aerobics, help to prevent the onset, and development, of this condition.

Other sports injuries

AQA	✓
EDEXCEL	✓
OCR	✓
WJEC	✓
CCEA	X

You should know the causes of winding, stitch and cramp.

Make sure you know how to spell hypothermia and hyperthermia. Mixing them up will lead to loss of marks.

Table 7.3 Injury: causes and symptoms

Injury	Causes and symptoms
Winding	Caused by a blow to the concentration of nerves in the upper abdomen called the **solar plexus**. This causes the diaphragm to go into spasm.
Stitch	A **pain** in the side of the abdomen or in the lower chest, brought on by physical activity. It is best described as a form of cramp in the diaphragm and restricts deep breathing.
Hypothermia	The result of the **lowering** of body temperature below 35ºC. When this happens the nervous system is affected, muscular rigidity can develop and the heart beats irregularly. Unconsciousness may follow. Hypothermia may occur in water-based and outdoor activities, e.g. canoeing and hill-walking.
Cramp	An **instantaneous contraction** of a skeletal muscle that cannot be relaxed. It can last for a few seconds or several minutes. Its precise cause is unknown, as muscle cramps occur during hard physical exercise or during complete relaxation. Causes are thought to be a lack of salt or minerals in the diet, or a temporary restriction of blood to the affected muscle.

Injury	Causes and Symptoms
Hyperthermia	Often referred to as **heat exhaustion**, it occurs when the body temperature rises above normal owing to excessive effort and dehydration. Shock and loss of co-ordination may develop. Hyperthermia may occur during long-distance running.
Shock	The result of **insufficient blood** circulating round the body. It is often caused by severe bleeding and / or severe pain. It shows itself in a number of ways: clammy skin, shallow and rapid breathing, a feeling of dizziness coupled with a desire to vomit and possibly with a lapse into unconsciousness.

Learn what may cause hypothermia and hyperthermia.

RICE formula

AQA	✗
EDEXCEL	✓
OCR	✗
WJEC	✗
CCEA	✗

For soft tissue injuries and other sporting injuries, when the casualty is conscious, treatment usually follows the **RICE** formula:

- **R – Rest** the injured part of the body at once.
- **I – Ice** should be applied to the affected part. This can reduce swelling and muscle spasm. It will restrict the flow of blood to the injured area.
- **C – Compression** needs to be applied to the injured area by means of an elastic bandage. This also helps to prevent swelling. Note that the bandage should not be so tight as to completely restrict the flow of blood.
- **E – Elevation** – the injured part needs to be raised. This should only be attempted if the movement does not cause pain.

Figure 7.2 The RICE formula

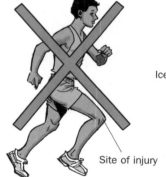
Site of injury

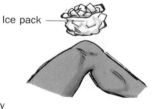
Ice pack

KEY POINT

Remember, any medical treatment should be carried out only by a qualified practitioner.

PROGRESS CHECK

1. Which three symptoms can usually be seen when inflammation at a joint occurs?
2. Explain the term 'osteoarthritis'.
3. What is the difference between hypothermia and hyperthermia?

1. Redness; Heat; Swelling.
2. Osteoarthritis is a form of arthritis caused by the wearing away of articular cartilage.
3. Hypothermia is when body temperature goes down to extreme levels; Hyperthermia is when body temperature goes up to extreme levels.

7.5 Specific sports injuries

LEARNING SUMMARY

After studying this section you should be able to understand:

- which injuries are most common to some sports

Specific sports injuries

AQA	✓
EDEXCEL	✓
OCR	✓
WJEC	✓
CCEA	✗

Many injuries are closely associated with certain sports, particularly body contact sports, such as rugby.

Some injuries will reflect the position that a person plays within a team. For example, in football, it would be expected that a goalkeeper would sustain different types of injuries from those of a striker. Participants in recreational activities, such as aerobics and keep-fit, can still pick up injuries, but of a different type from those of the games player (see Figures 7.3a–7.3d).

Figure 7.3a, Figure 7.3b, Figure 7.3c and Figure 7.3d Injuries associated with specific sports

Figure 7.3a Sports injuries associated with football

1. Pulled hamstring
2. Pulled calf muscle (gastrocnemius)
3. Fractured collar bone (clavicle)
4. Groin strain
5. Knee injury – torn ligaments, torn cartilage
6. Ankle injury – sprained ligaments

Figure 7.3b Sports injuries associated with aerobics

1. Strained ankle ligaments
2. Back pain and muscle strain
3. Groin strain
4. Strained muscles and tendons in upper leg and hip
5. Shin splints (stress fracture of tibia)

Figure 7.3c Sports injuries associated with cricket

1. Unconsciousness
2. Fractured ribs
3. Bruised and fractured toes
4. Fractures and bruising to forearms, hands and fingers
5. Bruised thighs
6. Pulled hamstrings

Figure 7.3d Sports injuries associated with basketball

1. Finger injuries
2. Groin strain
3. Jumper's knee
4. Sprained / dislocated thumb
5. Ankle strain
6. Jumper's heel

PROGRESS CHECK

1. What is a shin splint?
2. In cricket, what does a helmet aim to avoid?

1. A stress fracture to the tibia.
2. Unconsciousness / head injuries.

Sample GCSE questions

1 State **four** factors, which are part of the 1974 Health and Safety at Work Act, that are considered essential to safety in Physical Education.

All equipment must be safe to use.
The group size must be appropriate to the activity.
The ability of the group must match the event.
Activities and training sessions must be properly planned and controlled.
Safety equipment must be available and in good working order.
First aid must be available.
Procedures for calling in the emergency services must be in place.   **(4)**

Only four of these are asked for, but you should know them all.

2 **(a)** Give **two** reasons why jewellery should be removed when playing sport.

It can cut / hurt you / your opponent; It can distract the performer; It can get tangled and cause choking.   **(2)**

Only two suitable answers are needed. Any two of these would be suitable.

(b) What is the usual cause of chafing?

Ill-fitting clothing.   **(1)**

Just a simple answer is required.

3 Give the WHO definition of health.

WHO: World Health Organisation.

A state of complete physical, mental and social well-being, not just the absence of disease and infirmity.   **(3)**

You must know what WHO stands for in order to answer this question.

Exam practice questions

1 During a hockey match one of the female players slipped, fell over and injured her ankle. Apart from a sprain, what type of injury might she also have sustained?

....

.... **(1)**

2 Explain the difference between soft tissue injuries and hard tissue injuries.

....

....

.... **(2)**

3 Which of the following might **not** pose a personal hygiene problem?

Sweating ☐

Teeth ☐

Feet ☐

Legs ☐ **(1)**

4 Which of the following is **not** a potential hazard on a school playing field?

Broken glass ☐

Litter ☐

Painted lines ☐

Other players ☐ **(1)**

5 It is important to lift equipment properly. List **four** important factors to remember when lifting equipment on your own.

....

....

....

.... **(4)**

6 List **two** of the effects that obesity might have on the skeletal system.

....

.... **(2)**

8 Sport today

The following topics are covered in this chapter:

- **Leisure, recreation and sport**
- **Reasons for participation**
- **Factors affecting participation**
- **Modern technology**
- **The way we play**

8.1 Leisure, recreation and sport

LEARNING SUMMARY	After studying this section you should be able to understand:
	- what leisure is
	- how and why leisure time has increased

Leisure time

AQA	✓
EDEXCEL	✓
OCR	✓
WJEC	✓
CCEA	✓

We all have certain obligations, duties and needs. After these have been met, we often have some time left when we can do just what we want: we have a **freedom of choice**. This free time is called **leisure time** (see Figure 8.1).

Figure 8.1 The leisure time continuum

The Amount of Choice in Our Daily Lives

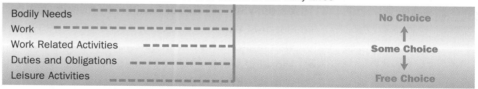

> **KEY POINT**
>
> Leisure time can be described as the time not needed to meet our social and bodily needs. Work / school are obligatory.

In this definition, our **bodily needs** include eating and sleeping, and work includes school or other full-time education. **Duties** and **obligations** vary from person to person. To mow the lawn could be classed by some as a duty, but to others, who enjoy such an activity, it could be classed as a leisure activity.

What people do in their leisure time varies. Many people spend their leisure time taking part in **recreational activities**. Recreational activities tend to be planned and may be physical activities.

Outdoor recreation describes activities that are followed in the country, in the natural environment. They include activities like walking, climbing and sailing. Lifetime sports describe those activities that a person may continue to do into old age. Bowls, badminton and swimming are good examples, whereas rugby definitely is not.

> **KEY POINT**
>
> Recreational activities can be defined as the activities that we choose to follow for their own sake.

People involve themselves in **physical recreation** activities for a number of reasons:

- **Physical benefits** – they help you to become fit and healthy.
- **Mental benefits** – they relieve stress and tension, are fun to do and make you feel better in yourself.
- **Social benefits** – they help you to meet people, make new friends and develop social skills, including consideration and appreciation of the needs of others.

Rules are needed in both physical recreation and sport.

Recreational activities often have **rules**, but these rules are sometimes less important than the fun of participation and they may not be adhered to fully. However, some rules are important for safety, whether playing is for fun or for competition. When the rules take on a major significance, and the competitive element of the activity becomes more important, then the recreational activity is referred to as a **sport**.

You must be able to distinguish between leisure, recreation and sport.

> **KEY POINT**
>
> A sport may be defined as an activity requiring physical prowess or skill, together with some hierarchical element, which results in a winner.

Increases in leisure time

People are getting more and more leisure time. This is due to the following:

You should be able to explain what has contributed to the increase in leisure time.

- **Working life** – the average adult's working life is now much shorter than it was 100 years ago. People do not start full-time work until at least 16 years of age (sometimes 21 or later if they go to university), and retirement age is currently 60 for women and 65 for men. In some jobs, retirement can come as early as 55. Better healthcare means that people live far longer. A hundred years ago, school ended at 11 years of age for many. Retirement was limited and few people retired with a pension.
- **Working week** – this has also reduced over the last 100 years. Compared with 45–50 hours worked per week 100 years ago, many full-time jobs today are for only 35 hours a week, often spread over a 5-day week. In addition, many people work shifts or restrict themselves to part-time employment.
- **Unwaged** – there is an increasing number of people who do not work at all. Some are unfortunate in that they cannot find a job, but others choose not to work, relying on a partner to support them. Many mothers and some fathers find that work is not an option if they have very young children.
- **Holiday time** – this has increased over the last 100 years, together with **paid holiday time**. Legislation giving all workers paid holiday time came into effect in 1938 and today many people have paid holiday time of up to 5 weeks, plus bank holidays.
- **Labour-saving devices** – these have become very popular and are now more efficient and affordable. Most homes have microwave cookers, washing machines, dishwashers and tumble dryers, which have all helped to reduce the time spent on household duties.

8.2 Reasons for participation

LEARNING SUMMARY	**After studying this section you should be able to understand:**
	• why people take part in sport
	• how sports participation has grown

Why people take part in sport

AQA	✓
EDEXCEL	✓
OCR	✓
WJEC	✓
CCEA	✓

Make sure you know the four main reasons why people take part in sport.

Most people who elect to play sport during their leisure time do so for a variety of reasons. For example…

- sport is enjoyable – it helps people to look good and feel good, and can give a sense of achievement. It can also stimulate aesthetic awareness.
- sport contributes to good health and aids recovery from illness. It also relieves stress and tension and may contribute to a longer life.
- sport is a social activity that encourages the development of friendships. It can help people learn how to work and play together as part of a team.
- sport can satisfy, in an acceptable way, the competitive element that is inherent in most people.

Growth of sports participation

Just as the amount of people's leisure time has increased, so has their active involvement in sport. This is due to a number of factors, often referred to as the 'PHEW' factors:

You should know the 'PHEW' factors that influence sports participation.

- **P – Peer pressure** – this is the influence that contemporaries have on each other. Individuals tend to be affected by group behaviour and if some of the group play sport, then others tend to take up sport as well. Gender also affects participation. Although more opportunities are now available for women to play sport, it is evident that more males than females play sport. Also, individuals like to follow fashion and, to many people, it is fashionable to play sport.
- **H – Home** – if parents play sport then they will also introduce their children to sport and encourage their participation in sporting activities. They will also help their children with the cost of specialist equipment and clothing. Ethnicity, tradition and cultural background can dictate whether an individual will take part in sport. Some cultures actively discourage females from taking part in sport.
- **E – Education** – schools have to teach sporting activities to all children through the National Curriculum. This provides children with a range of sporting skills and, hopefully, stimulates a lifelong interest in sport. A good PE teacher can develop a positive attitude to the benefits of taking part in regular sporting activities. The popularity of a specific sport can influence its inclusion in a school's programme.

● **W – Work** – the existing **socio-economic** climate will often dictate levels of participation. People who are unemployed or on a low income may be unable to finance sports participation. However, there has been an increase in the number of **job opportunities** in sports. More and more people are finding paid employment in sport, and there is a large number of **volunteers** who give their time to sport for free. Those who are paid include coaches, instructors, trainers and administrators. They will all have some acceptable **qualification** for the job that they do and will contribute to the increased participation in sport by the public at large. Many officials, such as judges, referees and umpires, work unpaid, but all are necessary if sport is to be made available to a large proportion of the population.

> **PROGRESS CHECK**
>
> ① What are the four main reasons why people take part in sport?
> ② Who tends to participate most in sport: males or females?
> ③ Who, in schools, often instils a positive attitude towards sports participation?
>
> 1. It is fun; It contributes to good health; It is a social activity; It satisfies a competitive need. 2. Males. 3. The PE teacher.

8.3 Factors affecting participation

> **LEARNING SUMMARY**
>
> **After studying this section you should be able to understand:**
> ● which factors can influence sports participation

Influencing factors

AQA	✓
EDEXCEL	✓
OCR	✓
WJEC	✓
CCEA	✗

Factors that affect an individual's participation in sport should not be confused with those that influence sport in a general way. Figure 8.2 shows those factors relating directly to the individual.

Figure 8.2 Influences on participation

> It is important that you know these factors and how they influence participation.

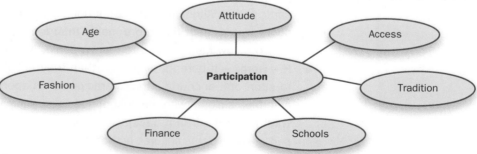

Age

Age is a big influence on the amount of time that a person has to spend on sports participation. As they get older, people participate in fewer and different activities. This is shown in Table 8.1. Figure 8.3 shows these changing trends in a visual form.

Table 8.1 Participation rates by age

Age range	Average participation in sport
Up to 16 years	Steady rise, large amount of time spent
18–30 years	Steady decline
30–50 years	Steady rise, sometimes more time spent than by teenagers
50 years	Gradual decline

Figure 8.3 Sports participation levels related to age

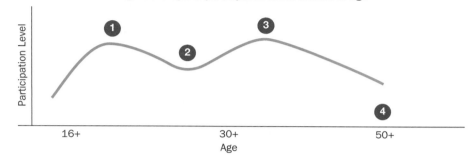

> Make sure you know the ups and downs of sports participation.

1 The first peak in Figure 8.3 reflects the period when young people, as students, have time to play sport and tend to benefit from concessionary rates at leisure / sports centres.

2 The first trough reflects the period when young people begin to spend more time and money on social activities, such as going out drinking with friends, and then on the establishment of a family life.

3 The second peak reflects the period when the whole family can take part in sport together, and then later as individuals.

4 The second trough reflects the period when people are getting older and looking for less-strenuous activities. This decline is more gradual than the first decline.

KEY POINT

Sport is not just for the young, but all age groups.

Attitude

Attitude is influenced, if not formed, by those most closely related to the individual.

KEY POINT

Tradition influences attitudes.

> If you play sport early in life, you will probably play sport all your life.

Parents who are active in sport encourage their children to be the same. They will expose their children to sporting traditions that will often be maintained in later life. This is not to say that children will always play the same sports as their parents, but they will have developed the sporting **ethos**.

Peer group acceptance is important to many adults and children alike. The desire to join in with groups can be very strong. What our friends do, we want to do. The advantage of this is that by joining one group of friends in sport, players are likely to meet, and make friends with, others who are also interested in sport.

Youth clubs and **specific sports clubs** make the young especially welcome. Club leaders hope that early participation in sport will help both the social and physical development of young children and will foster a future sporting tradition.

Access

The amount of time that can be spent on a sport depends to a large extent on the amount of sporting provision that is available locally. Schools tend to be well catered for, but this is not always the case for the general public. However, more and more local authorities are providing **leisure / sports centres** that can cater for individual and team activities. Such centres are often open all day, seven days a week, meaning that those in employment can benefit from their provision. Local sports centres may well provide concession cards for those on low incomes, and crèche facilities for mothers with young children.

> Note that some centres cater for single sports; most cater for a wide range.

Today, the vast majority of the population has access to sports facilities and few groups face restrictions. This has changed in the last 30 to 40 years; in the past, **women** were often denied the chance to take part in sports that were 'considered unsuitable'. Fortunately, this attitude has changed and now an increasing number of sports is available to all.

Fashion

Fashion has influenced, and no doubt will continue to influence, sports participation. The fun-running boom was started in the early 1980s and was fostered by local and national fun runs and city marathons. These events still take place today, with people running for fun and for charity, as well as for their own good.

> Note that aerobics is not a 'female' sport – it is just that few men try to do it.

A later development has been the rise in popularity of **aerobics** – especially **step aerobics**. This trend has caused an increase in female participation rates and has grown alongside the promotion of celebrity fitness videos, which encourage mainly women to look good, as well as feel good.

An often-underrated influence in the field of fashion has been the **clothing industry**. This industry has changed dramatically in its approach to **sportswear**. Sports clothing is no longer just functional; it has to be a **'fashion statement'**. It still has to do the job properly, but it also has to look good on the wearer. New materials and bright colours reflect the mood of the participants as they enjoy their sporting activities.

Finance

Money is probably the major ruling factor in sports participation. In general terms, if an individual cannot pay, then he / she cannot play. This is true with regard to privately run facilities, such as some golf clubs and health clubs. However, local authority provision is more sympathetic to those in difficult financial circumstances. **Concessionary rates** are often available for the young, the non-working or senior citizens (i.e. those who tend to be on a low or fixed income). **Governing bodies** often promote their sports at subsidised rates.

> Lack of funds should not prevent you participating, but it may govern where you participate.

The costs associated with the provision of facilities are now often met by a range of bodies, not just the user. Local Authorities, the Sports Councils, the National Lottery and industry (through **sponsorship**) all contribute towards the cost of sporting projects.

> You need to be aware of who can provide funds in sport.

Schools

Education plays a great part in our lives. All children and young people have to go to school. They also have to take part in sport or physical education. If this is well taught, the foundations for enjoying a healthy and sporting life will have been established. School sport should provide the confidence that is needed to take part in a range of sporting activities. (This topic is further developed in Chapter 11.)

> Do not forget the National Curriculum's role in sport.

Traditions

Traditions come from the area within which we grow up and live. They often develop over many years, reflecting the attitudes of specific communities and the geography of an area.

Up until a few years ago, the North of England was seen as the hotbed of rugby league, and few opportunities to get involved in the sport existed elsewhere in the country. Wales was considered to be a rugby union stronghold and Yorkshire a cricketing county.

In the past, sports often reflected the social class of the communities of the area. Working class communities were more likely to support football teams and rugby league, while rugby union was often seen as an upper-class sport. Country sports, such as golf, horse-riding and hunting, were also associated with the upper classes. Coastal areas have a strong tradition of water sports, while mountainous regions have seen climbing and hill-walking flourish. Lakeland areas support inland sailing and fell-walking.

Areas are proud of their sporting traditions and try to maintain them. However, the changes in attitudes to sports have, to some extent, broken down the traditional geographical and social distinctions related to a large number of activities.

PROGRESS CHECK

1. Give reasons for the decline in sports participation for the 18–30 age group.
2. When did fun runs and city marathons first become popular in this country?
3. Give examples of how geography affects sports participation.

1. They spend more money and time on social activities and the establishment of family life.
2. During the early 1980s. 3. Coastal areas support water sports; Mountainous areas support climbing; Lakeland areas support sailing / fell-walking.

8.4 Modern technology

LEARNING SUMMARY

After studying this section you should be able to understand:

- the influence of technological developments in training and sport
- the influence of ICT in modern sport

Technological developments

AQA	✓
EDEXCEL	✓
OCR	✓
WJEC	✗
CCEA	✗

There are many technological developments that have had both a positive, and sometimes a negative, influence on a wide range of sporting situations. These developments cluster in three main areas:

1. equipment
2. administration of events
3. digital images

1 Developments related to **equipment**:

- The use of **man-made fibres** in clothing has not only influenced fashion, but has had an effect on performance. They can keep performers warm, and help to prevent injury. Swimmers, in particular, are seen to wear suits that 'make them go faster'.
- **Safety equipment** is now made of stronger and lighter materials. Shin pads, head guards and cricketer's pads now offer more protection but do not hinder movement. Specialist footwear is designed for individual sports. Hockey goalkeepers have bigger, lighter protective equipment.
- The development of **graphite construction** for rackets, clubs and poles for vaulting allows performers to hit harder and stronger, and jump higher.
- Improved **landing areas**, such as rubber and foam mats in athletics and gymnastics, allow performers to land poorly without incurring injury, as well as giving them confidence to attempt great feats of performance. These improved landing areas assist greatly in the training of performers. Without them, styles such as the **Fosbury Flop** would not have developed (see Figure 8.4). After all, it is unnatural to want to land on the back.

2 Developments related to the **administration of events**:

- Improved **starting pistols** in athletics. These are now connected to **timing devices** and allow for accurate starts in races as well as more accurate timing of events.
- Touch pads along the wall of a swimming pool accurately record the finishing times and positions in a swimming race. The immersion of electrically operated equipment in water was, until recently, something that was not considered possible.
- The measuring of distances thrown is now calculated by **trigonometry** within a computer rather than by using tape measures. This is quicker and more accurate.
- **Recording sensors** fitted to shoes can tell officials where a competitor is in a race and if he has followed the wrong route. They are also attached to the end of foils and on body suits to register a hit in fencing (see Figure 8.5).

Figure 8.4 Improved landing area for the Fosbury Flop

Figure 8.5 Recording sensors fitted to fencing foil

3 Developments related to **digital images**:

- **Cameras** can show if a ball is in or out in a tennis match, and if a player is run out in cricket. They can provide **instant feedback** to help officials in decision making. A good example of this is the finish of a 100m event where the photograph shows the finishing order with times (see Figure 8.6).
- **Large screens** provide the spectator with better viewing of events on a pitch or within a stadium, and the instant displaying of results.
- Often, replays of actions can **call into question** the accuracy of an umpire's or referee's decision. As these replays may not be available for officials to use, they can **undermine** the credibility of the official and reduce his confidence in his future actions. For this reason, some do not see this as a beneficial development.

Figure 8.6 Digital image showing the end of a race

ICT

Aspects of **information** and **computer technology** are successfully applied to sporting situations. These include the following:

- **Monitors** – these are readily available to performers. Some can be attached to the chest to monitor heart rate, whilst others can measure power (see Figure 8.7).

Figure 8.7 A heart monitor in use

- **Computer programs** – these are used to track the performance of individuals and teams, helping to identify the strengths and weaknesses of players. Programs have been developed to assist officials with decision-making in cricket and tennis; they predict the flight path of the ball. In these sports, the Hawkeye program can be used to show if a person is run out in cricket or if the ball was 'in' in tennis. Commentators use it to predict the flight path of the ball in cricket to confirm or question the umpire's decision.
- **Visual analysis** – the use of playbacks to establish an analysis of movement patterns. This can help individuals to refine their skills (see Figure 8.8).

Figure 8.8 Back somersault

- **DVDs and CD-ROMs** – provide information and instruction in a wide range of sporting activities.
- **Websites** – these are the information providers for sports – for teams, clubs or individuals. In addition, interactive sites show examples of skill, performance, training and testing.

PROGRESS CHECK

1. Name some uses of graphite in sports.
2. In top class athletics events, what are starting pistols linked to?
3. What can be used to help performers to refine their skills?

1. To make rackets / clubs / poles stronger, thereby attaining greater distances or more height. 2. Timing devices. 3. Visual analysis.

8.5 The way we play

LEARNING SUMMARY	After studying this section you should be able to understand:
	• the way people take part in sport
	• behaviour patterns in sport

Competitions

AQA	✓
EDEXCEL	✓
OCR	✓
WJEC	✗
CCEA	✗

The three main types of competition are...
- league systems
- ladder systems
- knockout systems.

League systems are usually associated with **team** events. They will require each team to play all the other teams, sometimes on a home and away basis, with points being awarded for wins, draws and sometimes losses. If the final rank order of a league ends in a tie situation, then goal difference or points scored may be taken into account.

- Points are awarded for winning, e.g. 3 pts, and for drawing, e.g. 1 pt.
- Teams level on points may be separated by 'goal difference'.

Figure 8.9 An example of a league system – the ACME B Mid-Cheshire Motorway League

		P	W	L	D	F	A	GD	PTS
1	Sandbach	8	7	0	1	24	8	16	22
2	Middlewich	8	6	2	0	25	11	14	18
3	Kidsgrove	8	5	1	2	19	8	11	17
4	Biddulph	8	5	2	1	20	9	11	16
5	Alsager	8	4	2	2	16	13	3	14
6	Knutsford	8	4	3	1	14	13	1	13
7	Northwich	8	4	4	0	17	19	-2	12
8	Sale	8	2	1	5	11	12	-1	11
9	Alderley	8	3	3	2	10	14	-4	11
10	Stockton	8	1	5	2	6	17	-11	5

Ladder systems are often employed in **individual** sporting events, such as badminton or squash. Players are ranked in order of their ability so individuals can challenge players who are a limited number of places above them. Success means that a player takes the place of the beaten player, thereby moving up the ladder. Challenges can be made to those above, but must also be accepted from those below.

Figure 8.10 An example of a ladder system

1	A Player
2	S O Else
3	B A Newman
4	A Chance
5	M R Taylor

In some cases a player can challenge a player up to 3 places above. A successful challenge would result in all the players in between also moving down one place, as the winner takes over the higher place.

Knockout systems can be used for both team and individual competitions. They usually involve a 'draw' for the first round in order to select opponents, with the winner going through to the next round. After the first round, the draw follows one of two patterns. A second draw of the first round winners will take place to see who plays whom in the next round. This process will be repeated until the final is reached. This method is used in football's F.A. Cup competition. The alternative is for the winners from the first round to play an identified opponent in the next round. Winners from each round can see who their next opponent is likely to be (see Figure 8.11). The advantage of this is that some players / teams, usually the better ones, can be **'seeded'** to prevent them eliminating each other in the early rounds. This should ensure that the better players / teams meet in the later stages. This method is used at the Wimbledon Tennis tournament.

Figure 8.11 An example of a knockout system

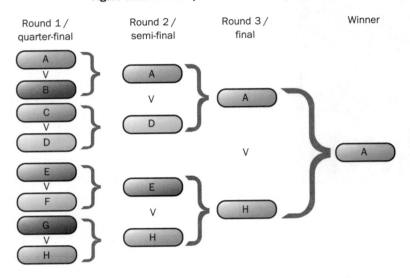

Sporting behaviour patterns

AQA	✓
EDEXCEL	✓
OCR	✓
WJEC	✗
CCEA	✗

Sporting behaviour is dictated by the way performers take part. Players must obey rules...

- to assist in the organisation and running of the game
- to ensure the safety of all concerned
- to add to the enjoyment of playing the game
- that are established by national organisations, but which may be adapted to meet local conditions.

It is the duty of all players to have a **thorough working knowledge** of the rules of the sport they intend to play. When playing the game, rule enforcement...

- must be **effective**
- must **be followed**, or else players can suffer some form of **penalty**, loss of points, free kicks or similar
- must not be **breached**, as this may result in the use of sin bins, suspensions, expulsions, bans or fines
- must be carried out **fully and fairly** to ensure the **safety** of players and to protect the **integrity** of the game.

Although **sports etiquette** is not, strictly speaking, a rule, it is expected during play. It is often referred to as the unwritten rule, which is a conventional form of behaviour, reflects **fair play** and good sporting attitudes, and is generally accepted as the 'way to play'. Fair play is also known as the **spirit of sportsmanship**. Unfortunately, it is often overlooked when a professional 'win at all costs' attitude is adopted.

PROGRESS CHECK

1. What type of sport best suits a ladder system?
2. In knockout competitions, what is the purpose of seeding?
3. What is often referred to as 'the unwritten rule' of sport?

3. Sporting etiquette.
2. To ensure that the better teams / players meet in the later rounds and do not eliminate each other at the start of the competition.
1. An individual sport, e.g. badminton, squash.

Sample GCSE questions

1 Explain how age can be a factor that influences participation in sport.

As people get older their bodies slow down, deteriorate and become less efficient. Therefore, they participate less in a sports activity, or change to a less demanding sports activity.

The very young are often physically undeveloped, therefore, some activities are unsuitable, e.g. contact sports. But some activities are more suited to the young, e.g. gymnastics.   **(5)**

Ensure you do not concentrate only on one age group.

2 Explain how education can be a factor that influences participation in physical recreation and sport.

All pupils must do PE at school and cover a range of activities. Many pupils experience extra-curricular sport. Both of these can influence a pupil's attitude to sport.

Good experience can encourage continued post-school participation.   **(3)**

When answering this type of question, try to lead from school activities to post-school activities.

3 Name the three most common ways of organising a sports competition. Give a sport that would suit each type of competition.

Ladder, e.g. badminton
League, e.g. football / hockey
Knockout, e.g. badminton / football   **(6)**

Although any sport can use the knockout system, the question asks for a sport to be named, so make sure you name one.

4 Give a definition of leisure time.

The time not needed to meet our social and bodily needs.   **(1)**

Exam practice questions

1   Explain how a local sports centre might provide for a number of groups from within the community.

....

....

....

.... **(6)**

2   How can each of the following factors influence participation in sport?

(a)   Personal finance ....

....

(b)   Tradition ....

.... **(4)**

3   Give **four** reasons why leisure time has increased over the last 100 years.

....

....

....

.... **(4)**

4   State whether each of the following sentences is **true** or **false**.

(a)   In top class athletics events starting guns are now connected to timing devices.

....

(b)   Graphite is used to strengthen rackets.

....

(c)   Body suits are worn as fashion clothing.

....

(d)   Rules are established by national organisations.

....

(e)   Visual analysis helps to improve skill.

....

(f)   Television cameras are not used at Wimbledon.

.... **(6)**

9 Participation

The following topics are covered in this chapter:

- **Discrimination in sport**
- **Status in sport**
- **Politics and sport**
- **Sporting behaviour**

9.1 Discrimination in sport

LEARNING SUMMARY

After studying this section you should be able to understand:

- gender discrimination in sport
- ethnic discrimination in sport
- disability discrimination in sport

The population of Great Britain originally developed from four major racial groups: English, Irish, Scottish and Welsh. Over the last 50 years or so, three major ethnic groups, namely Afro-Caribbean, Asian and Oriental, have added to the population. These racial identities are influenced by a range of religious beliefs, including the Roman Catholic, Muslim, Protestant and Jewish faiths. The sporting attitudes of these mixed racial / religious communities are also influenced by gender and disability.

Gender

AQA	✓
EDEXCEL	✓
OCR	✓
WJEC	✓
CCEA	✗

Traditionally, women did not have **equal opportunities** with men to participate in sporting activities. In the past, this reflected the views of many of the governing bodies of sport.

> **KEY POINT**
>
> The four major reasons why women's sport was originally held back were **clothing**, **class**, **motherhood** and **men**.

Clothing

There are many records of women taking part in a range of sports throughout the 19th Century, although they were often hampered by the clothes they wore (see Figure 9.1).

Figure 9.1 Ladies' hockey match, circa 1893

The first real piece of ladies' clothing for the then modern sportswoman was the culotte-style trousers pioneered by the American, **Fanny Bloomer**. These trousers, which became known as 'bloomers' or 'rationals', were designed with cycling in mind. This sport was a favourite of Queen Victoria and this royal patronage helped to promote cycling for women, though there is no evidence that the Queen ever wore a pair of fashionable bloomers. Before the advent of the bloomer, women tried to ride bicycles side-saddle – not very successfully.

At the turn of the last century, all respectable women were expected to wear an undergarment called a **corset**. This tight-fitting piece of clothing, made of whalebone, severely restricted movement. In 1919 the international tennis star, Suzanne Lenglen, shocked Wimbledon by playing tennis without her corset. Her fast movement about the court helped her to many successes. Lenglen and other women of this period were no doubt also helped by the invention and popularisation of the **brassiere** in the 1920s.

The development of less restrictive, more suitable sports clothing continued throughout the 20th Century and women's sportswear is now both fashionable and practical.

Class

Note that upper-class women had time for recreation, but lower-class women (the poor) did not.

The **status** of women in society has often dictated which sports they could participate in. In Victorian times, working-class women had little or no leisure time and, therefore, could not participate in much sport. Middle-class and upper-class women were encouraged to play games such as badminton and lawn tennis, but only at a simple recreational level. Their clothing would allow little running about. Class distinction has been progressively eroded, with many women now having both leisure time and financial resources in their own right.

Motherhood

Motherhood has always been the traditional role for a woman, who was expected to be the homemaker, to look after the children and elderly parents and act as the 'housewife'. This role persisted through a large part of the 20th Century. It is only recently that it has been accepted that women like Paula Radcliffe can combine the role of motherhood with that of being a top class sports performer.

> **KEY POINT**
>
> Women with children can play as much sport as those without children.

Note that campaigns are not always effective.

Although there are now more women taking part in more high-level sports than ever before, the number taking part at grass-roots level has been slow to increase. The Sports Council's campaigns, '**Sport for All**' in **1972** and '**Come Alive**' in **1977**, promoted equal opportunity but were not fully effective.

Note that this Act still reflects out-dated male attitudes towards women and sport.

The **Sex Discrimination Act of 1975** allows women to go to court if they feel that their rights are being abused in sport as well as in the workplace. However, the Act makes the concession that 'when the physical strength or stamina of the average woman puts her at a disadvantage to the average man – as a competitor – then discrimination can take place'. Unfortunately, many sporting bodies use this clause to encourage the separate development of men's and women's sport. However, many Sports Council grants are only awarded if the sport can show that discrimination no longer exists.

Despite these rather slow changes, women are taking part in more and more sports that were traditionally thought of as 'male' sports, for example, Cheryl Robertson, a Commonwealth kick-boxing champion and mother of two children; Jane Crouch, a world boxing champion since 1996; Wendy Toms, the first woman to officiate at a Premier League football match in 1997; and Dame Kelly Holmes, double gold Olympic medallist. Women have consistently beaten the world's best yachtsmen to win gold at several Olympic Games.

The **Women's Sport Foundation**, established in 1984, has done much to bring more women into the administration and coaching of sport.

Men

Men may have contributed most to the slow development of women's sport. Women have been poorly catered for in the modern Olympic Games, mainly because men felt that most events were 'too strenuous for women'. Women were not allowed to compete in the 1500m event until 1972, and the first women's marathon did not take place until 1984 at the Los Angeles Olympics.

> **KEY POINT**
>
> In the past, men always thought that they knew best, but they have been proved wrong many times in modern sport; women know just as much as men.

Men have consistently controlled the governing bodies of sports, and promoted sport as a male activity. An example of this was the attitude adopted by the Football Association, which refused to allow women's teams to affiliate to it and refused to recognise the Women's Football Association (established in 1969) until 1993. Even today, boys and girls over the age of 11 are not allowed to play the game together.

Sports where men and women do compete on equal terms include sailing and equestrian events, such as show-jumping. In these events women have repeatedly proved that they are not only equal to, but often better than, their male counterparts.

Ethnicity

AQA	✓
EDEXCEL	✓
OCR	✓
WJEC	✓
CCEA	X

Sporting fixtures have traditionally been held among the four home countries (England, Northern Ireland, Scotland and Wales) for many years and these serve to emphasise local national pride.

> **KEY POINT**
>
> Birthplace and skin colour have affected sports participation.

In the past, many sports discriminated against people because of their country of birth. If you were born in England, you could play only for England. This attitude has now changed and many sports allow a person to 'choose' their nationality through links with their parents' or grandparents' birthplace or by fulfilling a residency qualification.

At a county level, discrimination also often existed. In some sports a player could play only for the county in which he was born. But things have now changed. Some sports, such as professional cricket, allow each home county to play up to two registered overseas players alongside British-born players.

At professional club level, overseas players were not always made welcome by the spectators, and work permits, which allowed them to play in this country, were often refused. Professional football, however, had to change its attitude towards overseas players. The 1999 Bosman ruling by the European Court effectively said that any player from any E.U. country could play football for any club within the E.U.

Although the number of non-white players in a wide range of sports has increased, some resentment towards these players is still evident. Football has had to implement the campaign, '**Let's Kick Racism out of Football**', owing to the intolerant attitude of some spectators. Non-white groups often feel that they are isolated within Britain and, therefore, consider that they should support visiting teams playing against British sides.

> **KEY POINT**
>
> Birthplace and skin colour can still affect the pleasure of participation in sports for a large number of individuals in Britain today.

Disability

AQA	✓
EDEXCEL	✓
OCR	✓
WJEC	✗
CCEA	✗

> Disabilities can be physical and sensory. You should be aware of the difference.

To some people, sport is for people who are fit and healthy. To many, however, sport is for all – including those with a range of disabilities.

Today, the aim for the 'disabled' (also called the 'disadvantaged') is to show what they *can* do rather than what they *cannot* do.

In an effort to highlight some of the problems faced by disabled sportspersons, the United Nations nominated 1981 as the International Year for Disabled People. The aim was to encourage the provision of extra facilities for all disabled people in all walks of life. The Sports Council supported this with the campaign 'Sport for All – Disabled People'. This campaign aimed to encourage the provision of suitable sports facilities for the disabled, as well as encouraging the disabled to take part in sport. Today, no sports centre can be without access ramps, appropriate changing and toilet facilities, lifts and wider corridors suitable for people with disabilities.

The Paralympics now offer a wide range of events to compete in. Great Britain's Paralympians won a large number of gold medals in the 2008 Beijing Paralympics.

Figure 9.2 Competitor in a half-marathon

Religion

AQA	✓
EDEXCEL	✓
OCR	✓
WJEC	✗
CCEA	✗

> Be aware of the different religious beliefs followed in this country.

At first sight it would seem that sport has not suffered discrimination on religious grounds for many years. It is true that many of the top football clubs in Great Britain were founded as Protestant or Catholic church boys' clubs, which would not accept players from the other faith. Examples are Glasgow Rangers, Celtic, Liverpool and Everton. Today, such discrimination has largely disappeared. Even the Irish Olympic boxing team is drawn from boxers of all faiths.

Women who follow the Muslim faith are still restricted in the sports they can participate in. Their religion dictates their dress code, which in turn restricts participation. However, some attempts at change are being made.

Some individuals refuse to compete on a Sunday as they feel that this would go against their religious beliefs, and some largely Jewish football teams will not play games on Saturday, which is their Sabbath day.

PROGRESS CHECK

1. List the three main causes of discrimination in Britain today.
2. How did Fanny Bloomer help to increase participation in cycling in the 19th Century?
3. Name two Olympic events where men and women compete against each other on equal terms.

1. Gender; Ethnicity; Disability.
2. She invented culotte-style trousers for women, which became known as 'bloomers'.
3. Equestrian events (e.g. show-jumping); Sailing.

9.2 Politics and sport

LEARNING SUMMARY	**After studying this section you should be able to understand:**
	• some of the effects that politics have had on sport

The influence of politics in sport

AQA	✓
EDEXCEL	✗
OCR	✗
WJEC	✗
CCEA	✗

> Do you think sport and politics should be allowed to mix?

Sports can bind a nation together. It is possible that a population will combine to support a national sporting team in international competitions. This is one of the reasons why some governments have been prepared to use sport to further their own **political philosophies**. It is also the case that some sportsmen and women have used sport to **highlight specific political ideals**.

Sport has been used by many to draw attention to a range of aspects other than sporting prowess. The Olympic Games has been seen to be used many times by various governments and individuals to try to prove a political point.

You should be able to give examples of politics influencing national sports events.

Examples of political interference

Olympic Games	Interference
1936, Berlin, Germany	Hitler used the Games to further the Nazi cause. He **refused** to acknowledge the success of black US athlete **Jesse Owens**.
1956, Melbourne, Australia	**Spain** and **Holland** withdrew over the Russian invasion of Hungary. **Communist China** withdrew rather than compete against Taiwan.
1964, Tokyo, Japan	**South Africa's** invitation was withdrawn at the last minute because of Apartheid.
1968, Mexico City, Mexico	**Black US athletes** drew attention to poor civil rights back home with a **Black Power salute**. **South Africa** was refused admittance due to its political policies.
1972, Munich, Germany	**Rhodesia** (now Zimbabwe) was excluded after complaints about its treatment of black citizens. **Arab nationalists** took some of the Israeli team hostage, killing several. The hostage-takers were allowed to escape.
1976, Montreal, Canada	**South Africa** was still excluded. There was a **boycott** by many black African nations over the **New Zealand rugby tour** of South Africa.
1980, Moscow, Russia	The **USA** led a boycott by some western nations in protest over the **USSR** invasion of Afghanistan. Some UK athletes ignored the ban; others supported it.
1984, Los Angeles, USA	The USSR and some Eastern bloc countries boycotted the Games in retaliation for the USA actions in 1980. **Sponsorship** and **TV rights** funded the Games, which meant that the media influenced event times. Some athletes received payments for their success (amateur status having been dropped in 1981).

Of a more long-lasting nature was the expulsion of South Africa from the Olympic and Commonwealth movements in 1970, following pressure from many African countries who objected to the political régime of South Africa (Apartheid). The Gleneagles Agreement, signed in 1977, reinforced this ban and went on to say that countries should take steps to discourage sporting competition with South Africa until the political situation had changed. This was a direct use of sport to try to change the way an independent country governed itself.

Many countries also see the publication of the medal tables as an indication of their superiority over other nations.

Examples of political influences in Britain

Politics has had some positive influences on sport in Britain. For example:

- Finance – huge amounts of cash come directly or indirectly from central government.

Find out who the present Minister for Sport is.

- A National Lottery has been established, which includes sport as a good cause and worthy of special financial support.
- Organisation – a central government Sports Minister promotes the country's involvement in international sport and sets up a basic local sports structure.
- Provision – Acts of Parliament relating to sport have been passed, including the compulsory provision of sport in the National Curriculum.
- Legislation – laws control the safety standards of sporting venues and the care of young performers.
- Research – sporting disasters (e.g. Hillsborough) and youth sector involvement in sport have been investigated.
- Specific aid – governments support individual sports or organisations, such as the BOA, in staging international competitions (the most well-known being the 2012 Olympics bid).
- The protection of some events from commercial television ensures that sports such as the FA Cup Final and Wimbledon can be seen on 'free-to-view' television by anyone.
- The development of health-related programmes such as those aimed at obesity, alcohol abuse and AIDS.

PROGRESS CHECK

1. Which country was sent home from the 1972 Olympics?
2. When was the Gleneagles agreement signed and which country did it affect?

1. Rhodesia (now called Zimbabwe). 2. 1977; South Africa.

9.3 Status in sport

LEARNING SUMMARY

After studying this section you should be able to understand:
- the effects that differing types of sports performers have on sport

Status in sport

AQA	✓
EDEXCEL	✓
OCR	✗
WJEC	✗
CCEA	✗

Playing for pay

Most people participate in sport for enjoyment alone. Others want to supplement this enjoyment with financial rewards. This has led to a number of categories of players:
- Amateurs – simply play for fun and take no pay.
- Professionals – play for money: to them this is just a form of employment, a job.
- Semi-professionals – have a job, but are also paid to play sport on a part-time basis.
- Shamateurs – claim to be amateurs, but do in fact get paid for playing.

Status

Players are only eligible to take part in certain types of competition. Open competitions are for all types of player – amateur to professional. Amateur competitions are open only to genuine amateur players. Standards vary, but as more competitions become open the standard steadily rises. In 1968 Wimbledon became the first grand slam tennis tournament to go 'open'.

Changes to status

Over the past 30 years the financial rewards to players have undergone several changes. In the past...

- rules relating to payment were 'bent' by players and officials
- players received payments whilst claiming amateur status
- the establishment of Trust Funds allowed amateur players to get cash prizes, put the cash in a fund and use it only for training purposes, being able to draw on the residue in post-competition days
- dubious forms of employment were often given to amateurs
- some colleges and universities in the USA offered sports scholarships so that students could train full-time
- some countries, especially communist countries, drafted talented performers into the armed forces, therefore allowing them to train full-time, yet retain their amateur status
- valuable gifts were given to winners of events, which could then be traded for cash
- illegal payments, often called 'boot money', were common in many sports especially rugby union. Players came off the field to find cash in their shoes!

Most sports now embrace payments. The distinction between amateur and professional has become very blurred. Amateurs and professionals play alongside, or in competition with, each other. This has contributed to the raising of standards in some sports – men's sports in particular. Women's sports tend to attract less professionalism, possibly due to their reduced coverage in the media.

> **PROGRESS CHECK**
>
> 1. Explain the term 'semi-professional'.
> 2. Explain the term 'shamateur'.
> 3. Why do women's sports tend to have fewer professionals?
>
> 3. Because of reduced media coverage.
> 2. A player who claims to be an amateur, but receives payment for playing.
> 1. A player who is paid to play, but also has another job.

9.4 Sporting behaviour

LEARNING SUMMARY	After studying this section you should be able to understand:
	• group and individual behaviour patterns related to sport

Behaviour

AQA	✓
EDEXCEL	✓
OCR	✗
WJEC	✗
CCEA	✗

Behaviour can be both good and bad. The beneficial feature of sport, especially competitive games, is that it provides an emotional outlet to relieve tensions and control aggression. Playing within the rules of the sport involves sporting etiquette, respect and courtesy for both opponents and the game. These attitudes are examples of good behaviour related to sport.

Unfortunately bad behaviour, or **anti-social** behaviour, is all too evident in sport. This can be seen as...

- **over-aggression**, e.g. deliberate foul play, intentional fouling, committing so-called 'professional fouls'
- **gamesmanship**, e.g. time-wasting, diving, trying to 'fool' the referee
- **cheating**, e.g. using unfair tactics, drugs
- **sledging**, e.g. trying to disrupt the opposition by making adverse comments, trying to 'psych out' the opponent or break his concentration
- **intimidation of officials**, e.g. repeated challenging and commenting on decisions, in order to raise doubt in the minds of officials and possibly put them off their job
- **adverse spectator behaviour**, e.g. swearing at, and giving abuse to players, officials and visiting fans.

Spectators can have their good points. For example, they can influence the outcome of a match by giving **positive support** like cheering on their own team, which makes playing at home an advantage. They give **financial support** to their team or club by buying tickets, club merchandise and often social membership of the club.

However, spectators can also have their bad points. For example, they may **intimidate** visiting players, officials and other spectators from the sidelines. This can cost the home club extra expense for marshals and an increased police presence to keep order. Such anti-social behaviour can spill over to the streets outside the ground, causing damage to property and injury to people. This type of behaviour is referred to as **hooliganism**. It is often fuelled by **alcohol**, **racism** and **misplaced loyalty** and has been a feature of many football matches both at home and abroad.

Football hooliganism became a major concern in Britain during the 1970s and 1980s, but is still evident today. Two tragedies – **Heysel** in 1985 and **Hillsborough** in 1989 – led to a government enquiry to establish causes of hooliganism, ways to combat violent crowd behaviour, control crowd movement and how to prevent future tragedies. This enquiry, which became known as the **Taylor Report** after the name of its chairman, made a number of recommendations. These included...

- the removal of perimeter fences and the provision of all-seater stadia
- the segregation of fans
- the use of CCTV both inside and outside grounds
- the sharing of intelligence about troublemakers between different police forces
- the control of sales of alcohol within and close to the ground.

PROGRESS CHECK

1. What does sport provide emotional outlets for?
2. What is meant by 'sledging' at a sports match?
3. Name the report set up to prevent possible future tragedies at sports grounds.

3. Taylor Report.
2. Trying to disrupt an opponent's concentration by making adverse comments and breaking concentration.
1. Tensions and aggression.

Sample GCSE questions

1 What are disabled sportspersons now more often known as?

Disadvantaged. **(1)**

2 Give **three** ways in which people with disabilities can be encouraged to use leisure facilities.

Wider corridors / aisles; Improved changing facilities; Installation of lifts; Installation of ramps. **(3)**

There are a number of reasons that can be given but the question only asks for three, so any three of these would be satisfactory.

3 Name **two** sports in which women repeatedly beat men in the Olympic Games.

Sailing and horse-riding. **(2)**

4 What are the four main reasons why women's sports were originally held back?

Clothing, class, motherhood and men. **(4)**

You should be able to explain these if asked to.

5 Why was the invitation to the 1964 Olympics withdrawn from South Africa?

Because of the political situation in the country at that time (Apartheid). **(2)**

You must be able to describe the features of Apartheid, and be aware of the many influences of politics on the Olympic Games.

Exam practice questions

1 Explain how the Olympic Games have encouraged the development of sport for the disabled.

....

....

....

.... **(3)**

2 Explain how political and international problems affected the Olympic Games in 1968 and 1972.

....

....

....

.... **(4)**

3 Which of the following are examples of bad behaviour?

Over-aggression ☐

Cheating ☐

Sledging ☐

Skiing ☐ **(2)**

4 What are the main recommendations of the Taylor Report?

....

....

....

....

.... **(6)**

10 Media and sponsorship

The following topics are covered in this chapter:

- **Types of media**
- **Media presentation**
- **Effects of the media**
- **Sponsorship in sport**

10.1 Types of media

LEARNING SUMMARY

After studying this section you should be able to understand:

- the written coverage of sport
- the broadcast / electronic coverage of sport

Types of media coverage

AQA	✓
EDEXCEL	✓
OCR	✗
WJEC	✓
CCEA	✗

Media	Audience	Type of Coverage
Videos / Film		Recorded entertainment (best action). Educational (coaching series).
Books		Stories behind events, Biographies – for leisure or education.
Magazines		Specialised or general – informative and educational.
Internet		Fast information access. Possibly educational and / or entertaining.
Radio		Informative and entertaining with results, reports, comments, etc.
Newspapers (Tabloid and broadsheet)		Informative – results, reports, balanced views, opinions, etc. Entertaining – sensational stories, private lives exposed. Educational – tips to develop skills, fitness.
Television (Terrestrial – licence fee. Satellite, Cable, Digital, Interactive – all subscription or pay-per-view)		Informative – results, reports, comment, text, live action, highlights. Entertaining – live action, highlights, specialised programmes. Educational – documentaries, coaching series, live action, highlights, specific programmes for schools.

Written coverage

Written coverage includes **newspapers**, **magazines** and **books**. These three types of written media report or comment on sport in some way. The information they contain is usually at least 24 hours old. Print media can never report immediately on sport, as television can.

Newspapers

All newspapers contain substantial coverage of sports, usually on the back pages, and many include special supplements. Sports are reported, illustrations are given, actions are commented on and opinions are expressed.

Reports should be **factual** and **objective**, but this is not always the case. Regional and local newspapers in particular will often present a biased viewpoint (e.g. 'our side lost' not 'the visiting opposition won'). Often, excuses for losing are given.

Illustrations should reflect the action of the game, but this is not always so. Pictures of males tend to show their skills in the game or reflect their efforts in performance. The pictorial coverage of women, however, is not always so objective. What a female is wearing or what she looks like is often highlighted and the pictures may well concentrate on the female form or the under-garments worn, rather than her skill.

The actions of players, particularly those that can be **sensationalised**, regardless of whether they reflect the game, often take pride of place. Players' efforts are often underestimated, particularly if the local side lost. **Opinions** are often expressed by those who have only a limited knowledge of the game and are often based on supposition rather than fact. If newspapers are so lacking in professional objectivity, why do they put so much effort into covering sports events?

> Mostly national newspapers tend to sensationalise; local newspapers tend to lack objectivity.

KEY POINT

The reason for giving sports coverage is that sport helps to sell newspapers.

The fact that sport helps to sell newspapers is reflected in the range of sports covered. Soccer and racing in the winter and cricket and racing in the summer are the main sports in some newspapers (unless it is an Olympic year). Some do carry a wider range of sports but few give equal coverage to less popular sports or women's sports.

Magazines

Magazines cover a wide range of sporting activities and are often fully illustrated, but the news they carry can be over a week old. Most magazine coverage tends to be specialised: each publication relates to a specific sport. Because of this, a wide range of topics related to the sport can be covered and, more importantly, less popular sports often have their own weekly or monthly publication. Sports-specific magazines tend to be more knowledgeable and reliable than newspapers.

Books

Books come in a number of different styles. There is a wealth of autobiographical / biographical publications, especially from the more popular sports such as football, racing and rugby, especially if the writer is a well-known personality. Other books tend to be of an educational nature: they help people learn to do a sport or obtain a qualification in it.

Broadcast / electronic coverage

Broadcast / electronic coverage includes **films** and **videos**, **radio**, **television** and the **internet**.

Radio and television

> **KEY POINT**
>
> Radio and television, unlike film or video, can be instant. Play can be watched, or listened to, as it happens, where it happens and how it happens, all around the world.

Instant replays can provide the basis for comments and analysis, and viewers and listeners can form their own opinions on live performances.

Note that much of the broadcast word is linked to sponsorship.

The advent of many commercial television channels has increased the amount of sport shown and, therefore, many of the less well-known sports are now getting more publicity.

The internet

The internet is an **exploding aspect** of the media. Facts, comments, illustrations and information of all types can be broadcast on the internet. The sites are sometimes 'official', generated from a credited source, e.g. the official Sport England site. Others appear without accreditation and often include information that is of doubtful veracity or that may be pure gossip. Unfortunately, websites cannot be controlled in the way that other aspects of the media can.

> **PROGRESS CHECK**
>
> 1. What are the three main areas of the written word?
> 2. What is the basic fundamental difference between the written word and the broadcast / electronic word?
> 3. Which part of the media allows you to form your own opinions of the sporting action and why?
> 4. Which aspect of broadcast coverage cannot be controlled?
>
> 4. The internet.
> 3. The live broadcast, because you can see or hear it as it happens.
> 2. The written word is at least 24 hours old. The broadcast / electronic word is mainly live.
> 1. Newspapers; Magazines; Books.

10.2 Media presentation

LEARNING SUMMARY	**After studying this section you should be able to understand:**
	• broadcasting rights related to sport
	• which sports are presented on television

Broadcasting rights

AQA	✓
EDEXCEL	✓
OCR	✗
WJEC	✓
CCEA	✗

Broadcasting rights apply largely to television coverage, but also to some radio coverage of sporting events.

In order to broadcast a sporting event, a television company must purchase the **broadcasting rights**. The money is often paid to the governing body of the sport but part or all may be paid to those competing. The FA (Football Association) may sell the rights to a football match and share the proceeds with the teams involved. Two boxers, however, could share the entire payment between them. These rights may be to show the event once only, or as often as the television company wants. The television company might sell on part of the rights to other broadcasters who may want to show part of an event, such as highlights only. If a company buys **exclusive rights** then only that company can broadcast the event.

> By selling rights, the event becomes a product, not just a sport.

KEY POINT

Companies buy broadcasting rights to make money out of them, not necessarily to support the sport.

Some **satellite television** companies have tried to buy up the rights to all the most interesting and exciting sporting events. Because these companies often charge viewers to see the event, they can afford to pay a higher price than the terrestrial companies, such as the BBC, which show events without specific charge other than the annual television licence fee.

> Sports in the free-to-view list may change and be included on some digital channels. Your teacher should be able to keep you up-to-date on these changes.

There was a danger that all the best matches and coverage of the most popular sports would be available only to those who could afford to pay extra to watch them. So, in 1996, the **Broadcasting Bill** was passed, which decreed that some sporting events should be made available to all companies so that any viewer could watch them. These events include the **FA Cup Final** and **Wimbledon** and are shown by the BBC or ITV. This was good news for those viewers who do not want to pay, but it could be depriving the events of a much-needed income.

Sports on television

> Note that all these are male-orientated sports.

In the 1950s, before independent television was fully established, the BBC broadcast only a limited number of sporting events. These included cricket, football and tennis. To counteract this monopoly, the developing ITV companies offered a different range of sporting events. These included horse-racing, rugby league and wrestling, which became a national favourite in the 1960s and 1970s.

The controlling bodies of sport soon realised that television coverage of a sport meant that it would become more popular and more people would participate in it. The more people who participated in a sport, the greater their interest in that sport, meaning they would want to see more of their sport on television.

KEY POINT

Television coverage can increase the popularity of a sport.

> Remember that sports also aim to make money out of television companies.

Today, wherever possible, sports sell themselves to the highest bidder for a limited period only. Many television companies try to broadcast as much sport as possible, but only a few get the chance to show the major events. With more time available to show sports, a wider range of sports is being broadcast. Certainly a wide range of men's sports is shown – most women's sports still do not get a large amount of air time.

10.3 Effects of the media

LEARNING SUMMARY	After studying this section you should be able to understand:
	• the positive effects that the media can have on sport
	• the negative effects that the media can have on sport

Positive effects of the media on sport

AQA	✓
EDEXCEL	✓
OCR	✗
WJEC	✓
CCEA	✗

Of all aspects of the media, television has the biggest impact on sport. The most important contribution that television makes to sport is money.

Figure 10.1 Sports–television loop

KEY POINT

More television cash = More popularity. With popularity comes a large slice of advertising revenue.

Figure 10.2 Sports popularity double-loop

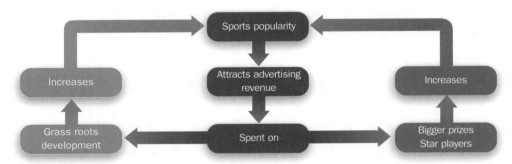

In addition to cash, television has influenced the rules of some sports and the times that those sports are played. For example, football can now be seen live throughout the week, which is an advantage to fans.

Rule changes are designed to increase the interest and excitement of a sport, and bring about quicker results. This is illustrated with the introduction of the **tie-breaker** rule in tennis. It speeds the game up, makes it easier to follow and generates more interest.

In addition, television educates the viewers, as they learn the rules of the sport from good commentaries, and greater understanding leads to more interest in the sport. Another spin-off from this increased wealth gained by TV coverage is that sports can provide better coaching and training for young players. This increases the overall standard of play in the sport and helps to create more interest in it.

Figure 10.3 Influences on sport of money generated by TV coverage

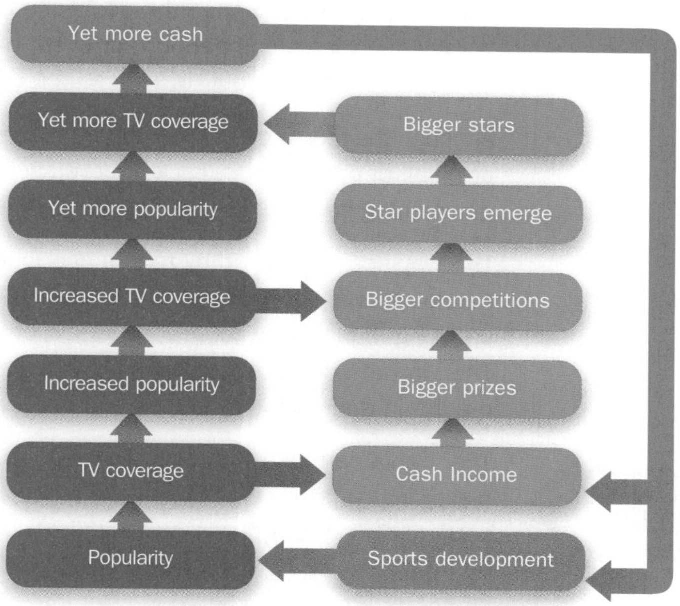

TV coverage gives players 'star' or 'celebrity' status, allowing them to gain greater income from outside the sport, for example, through **product endorsement** and sponsorship (almost invariably of male-orientated products). So, most of the stars produced in this way are male sportsmen who can act as positive role models for younger players. Unfortunately, few women are accorded this status.

Continually improving **technological innovations** result in better coverage and analysis of sport, creating feedback for players, coaches, officials and the public. These developments help to increase audiences, often on a worldwide basis, resulting in improved sponsorship opportunities.

Negative effects of the media on sport

AQA	✓
EDEXCEL	✓
OCR	✗
WJEC	✓
CCEA	✗

Just as the media contributes to the positive side of sport, it can also make negative contributions. The media wants **maximum exposure** of an event and can, therefore, influence the time and date when an event will take place. It can demand **personal appearances** and interviews and even dictate which sponsorship logos are given **exposure** during these interviews.

> **KEY POINT**
>
> TV needs sport, as it is popular with viewers, but TV will only buy broadcasting rights on certain terms.

If a sport wants to get television coverage it must increase its suitability for a TV audience that is not always concerned with the skills of the sport. For example, if female beach-volleyball players do not wear skimpy costumes, then they will not be shown on TV and the sport will lose popularity. The costumes, however, do not increase the skill level in the game.

A sport needs TV coverage to increase its popularity and to make money to spend on itself.

The repeated showing of **contentious issues** can undermine officials and call into question their abilities within a given sport. Indeed, **instant feedback** can be used by players to change the decisions of officials, as is seen at the Wimbledon tennis competition, or even to make the decision for the officials as in the case of a 'run out' in Test Match cricket.

Although the media can increase the popularity of a sport, it can also bring about the downfall of other sports. Lack of coverage can reduce a sport's popularity, thereby diminishing its potential for sponsorship, and the sport may then go into decline.

The way sport is played by teams and individual players can be affected by the media. A **'win at all costs'** approach can develop forms of gamesmanship or cheating in players who see the result of the game as a 'life or death' situation. This, in turn, can create **intense rivalry** between groups of spectators, which results in anti-social behaviour and hooliganism.

Some spectators love to hate some sports stars.

The media can also affect the **status** of performers within a sport. It can make a player into a 'star', but it can also break a player. It can intrude into the personal life of the player and highlight, or exaggerate, sensational stories in the name of 'news'. Perhaps the biggest fault of the media is that it does not treat all sports equally. Some sports get lots of coverage, a great deal of money and, therefore, increased popularity. Others, for a number of reasons, are virtually ignored.

Sport makes money out of television, and television makes money out of sport, but who gains most is open to question.

PROGRESS CHECK

1 What are the two major benefits to sport of television coverage?
2 What can television coverage do for good sports players?
3 In what ways do television companies dictate to sporting bodies?

1. Increased popularity; Cash. **2.** It can make them into stars / celebrities. **3.** The timing of events, rule changes, clothes to be worn.

10.4 Sponsorship in sport

LEARNING SUMMARY	After studying this section you should be able to understand:
	• what sponsorship is
	• the ways in which sponsorship can operate

Sponsorship

AQA	✓
EDEXCEL	✓
OCR	✗
WJEC	✗
CCEA	✗

Sponsorship is a **commercial transaction** that provides financial and material support within sport.

The sport (and / or the player) acts as an advertising site for certain products in return for financial or material support. By providing this support, the product receives publicity through its association with the sport, club or player.

Table 10.1 Types and recipients of sponsorship

Recipients of sponsorship	Types of sponsorship
• A **sport**, e.g. Amateur Swimming Association • A **team**, e.g. any Premiership football team • An **event**, e.g. World Snooker Championship • A **competition**, e.g. the Super League (Rugby League) • An **individual**, e.g. personal contracts with sportswear companies	• **Money** for living expenses. • **Kit and equipment**, e.g. sportswear, tennis racquets, etc. • **Travel**, e.g. a car. • **Scholarships** to attend a centre of excellence. • **Food** to help with sport-specific diets.

KEY POINT

Sponsorship, advertising and the media are closely linked. They can all exert pressure on a sport.

Operation of sponsorship

Some sports attract more sponsors than others. The minority sports find it much harder to attract 'big money' sponsors.

Figure 10.4 Wheels of sponsorship

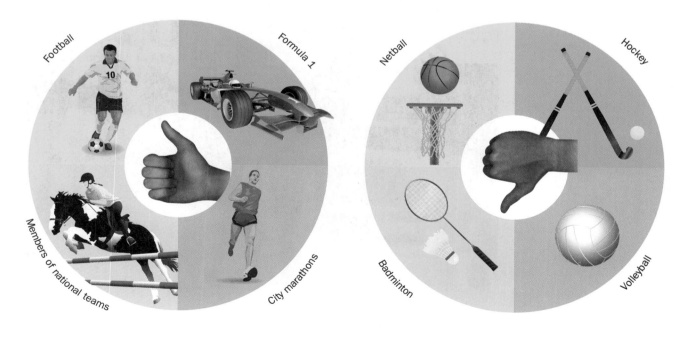

There are advantages and disadvantages of sponsorship deals. These can be summed up as shown in Table 10.2.

Table 10.2 Advantages and disadvantages of sponsorship deals

	Advantages	Disadvantages
For the sport, individual or event	• **Aids development** of young potential stars. • **Reduces financial pressure**, enabling training and competing to be full time. • **Funds events** by covering the organisational and administrative costs. • **Provision** of coaching, equipment, travel, specialist facilities, etc. • **Increased income** resulting in superstar salary status.	• **Exploitation** to suit the sponsor's needs. • **Length of contract** may be short, which provides less security. • **Support may be withdrawn** if the sponsor's income becomes reduced. • **Minority sports may decline** as major sports attract most sponsorship. • **Wrong image presented** through tobacco or alcohol sponsorship.
For the sponsor	• **Success / health / popularity** is associated with the sponsor. • **Media coverage** is a powerful advertising outlet. • **Logos or brand names** become well known and recognised. • **Often tax deductible** – can be set against profits to reduce tax.	• **Risk element** since success in sport is not guaranteed. • **Media coverage** may reduce or even cease. • **Wrong image presented** – with hooliganism at events – by poor behaviour of individual or team sponsored.

PROGRESS CHECK

1 List three sports that get little sponsorship.
2 What do sports **not** want the media to cover?

1. Any suitable answers, for example: Netball, hockey, badminton.
2. The wrong image, such as hooliganism.

Sample GCSE questions

1 Name **one** terrestrial television channel that shows sport.

BBC 1   (1)

Other correct answers could be: BBC2, ITV; Channel 4; Channel 5.

2 Suggest **two** reasons why most sports shown on television are male-dominated sports.

Tradition - sport was always seen as a male preserve.
Commercialism - male sports sell more goods.
Role models - there are more male than female role models from sport.
Spectacular performances - male sports are seen as more spectacular.   (2)

Be specific and explicit in your answers. Four reasons are given here, but only two are asked for. Any two of these reasons would be acceptable. Make sure you give a brief explanation with each reason given.

3 *Rugby World, Golfer* and *Triathlete's World* are just three of the many specialist sports magazines published regularly.

Suggest **three** reasons why magazines such as these are popular.

They are specific to the sport - they cater for a specific target readership.
They tend to deal with up-to-date topics.
They contain a great deal of information about the sport.
They are often good sources of reference for the sport.
They give details about role models and stars of the sport.   (3)

Any three of these reasons would suffice. Again, be specific with your three reasons.

4 Using examples to help you, discuss both the advantages and disadvantages of sponsorship deals for an individual and a sport.

Advantages - aids development, reduces financial pressure, funds events, increases income.
Disadvantages - exploitation, length of contract, support may be withdrawn, minority sports may decline, wrong image may be presented.   (6)

Cover both aspects of the question and explain the points made. Be aware that six marks would be given for six facts.

Exam practice questions

1. Give **one** reason why famous sportspeople are used to promote products in the media.

   ....

   .... **(1)**

2. Give **two** ways in which 'instant feedback' can affect decision-making in a sport.

   (a) ....

   (b) .... **(2)**

3. List **three** ways in which 'technological innovations' have affected sports development.

   (a) ....

   (b) ....

   (c) .... **(3)**

4. Describe the five major recipients of sponsorship and the five major types of sponsorship that each might receive.

   ....

   ....

   ....

   ....

   .... **(10)**

11 Organisation and provision of sport

The following topics are covered in this chapter:

- School and sport
- Structure of sport
- Funding of sport
- Providers of sport

11.1 School and sport

LEARNING SUMMARY

After studying this section you should be able to understand:

- how sport is promoted in school
- the opportunities available
- PESSYP and PESSCL

School and sport

AQA	✓
EDEXCEL	✓
OCR	✗
WJEC	✓
CCEA	✓

Many young people get their first introduction to sporting activities at a very early age through parents and friends. However, their first more formal, structured involvement in sport comes in their school life.

Schools encourage participation in a number of ways, for example...

- **compulsory lessons** are part of the **National Curriculum** and include **individual and team games**, **gymnastics**, **athletic activities**, **dance** and **swimming**
- **extra-curricular activities**, which include school clubs in a range of sports; **representative** honours for school, district or higher levels; **residential** experiences; the use of local community facilities; out-of-school club links and specialist coaching.

Not all sports work in school is done by a PE department alone. The importance of fitness within a healthy lifestyle and healthy living is often promoted through school **health education programmes**, **food technology**, **science** and **pastoral (PSE)** work. The way to attain the appropriate healthy lifestyle will vary with the type of occupation that students may eventually follow – sedentary, manual or outdoor. Links with **ICT** and **drama** are also commonplace.

Many schools provide opportunities for students to be involved in sport at more than a performance level. Supporting knowledge will be offered so that students can experience the roles of **trainer**, **coach**, **choreographer**, **leader** and **official**. Much of the extra-curricular work will depend upon the attitude of teaching staff and the availability of specialist coaching staff.

Sporting opportunities

Schools provide the first opportunities for qualifications within sport. These can be simple or more complex **achievement awards**, and **coaching** and **sports leadership** courses (see CCPR and CSLA on page 143). There is a wide range of public examinations available through a number of educational establishments. **GCSE** and **A-level** work might be offered through school or college. **BTEC** and **GNVQ** courses are more often found in colleges. Many of these courses may form the preparation for degree courses in a number of sports-related subjects, which are usually offered by universities.

PESSYP

PESSYP stands for **Physical Education and Sport Strategy for Young People**. It is often referred to as the '**5 Hour Offer**'. The aim of this strategy is, by 2011, to give all pupils 5 hours of sport every week. This will consist of 2 hours of quality PE within the school curriculum and a further 3 hours outside the school day in clubs or in other community opportunities. The **Youth Sport Trust** looks to enhance the quality of PE in a number of settings, and promotes the **TOP Link** programme, which encourages 14–16 year olds to organise sport in local primary and special schools.

PESSCL

PESSCL stands for **Physical Education, School Sport and Club Links**. It is a central government initiative aimed at encouraging sports participation by the young. It aims to encourage and foster club–school links through the development of **specialist sports schools / colleges** and **school sports co-ordinators**. These, in turn, will help to develop students who are gifted or show they have a potential talent, guiding them towards high quality, accredited sports clubs.

PESSCL looks to increase the number of young people playing sport and focuses on **Club Accreditation Programmes** – nationally recognised achievement awards.

PROGRESS CHECK

1. What does PESSYP stand for?
2. What does PESSCL stand for?

1. Physical Education and Sport Strategy for Young People.
2. Physical Education, School Sport and Club Links.

11.2 Structure of sport

LEARNING SUMMARY

After studying this section you should be able to understand:

- how sport is organised at a local level
- how sport is organised at a national level
- how sport is organised at an international level

Local organisation of sport

AQA	✓
EDEXCEL	✗
OCR	✗
WJEC	✓
CCEA	✓

To take part in a sport it is not essential, but is most useful, if an individual is a member of a sporting club. The pathway to representing your country in a sport is shown in Figure 11.1.

Figure 11.1 Organisational structure of competitive sport

International Competition

National Competition

County Competition

Regional Competition

Club Competition

Individuals

KEY POINT

To take part in international competitions you must belong to a local sports club.

All local sports clubs have several things in common:

- They are run by the members for the members.
- They organise facilities and competitions.
- They administer the paperwork of the club.
- They control the membership of the club.

> You must know the functions of a local sports club.

Most local sports clubs have a similar structure, as shown in Figure 11.2:

Figure 11.2 Structure of local sports clubs

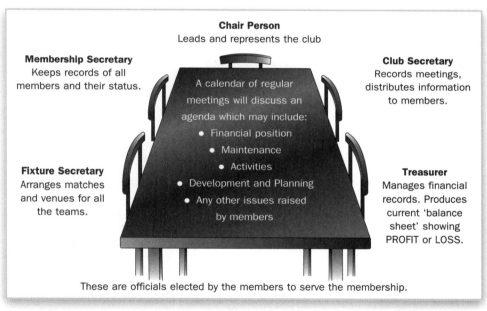

Chair Person
Leads and represents the club

Membership Secretary
Keeps records of all members and their status.

Club Secretary
Records meetings, distributes information to members.

A calendar of regular meetings will discuss an agenda which may include:
- Financial position
- Maintenance
- Activities
- Development and Planning
- Any other issues raised by members

Fixture Secretary
Arranges matches and venues for all the teams.

Treasurer
Manages financial records. Produces current 'balance sheet' showing PROFIT or LOSS.

These are officials elected by the members to serve the membership.

> You should know the duties of both club members and officials.

When a player joins a club, he / she accepts a responsibility towards the other players and organisers of the club, to play and support the club to the best of their ability. By the same token, the officers (president, secretary and treasurer) of the club have a responsibility to the players to organise the club so that each individual can play the sport.

Local sports clubs offer competitive, recreational and social events alongside coaching and sports development opportunities. They look to develop talent within their own club and also in the wider community. Local sports clubs are part of the community: they often draw resources from the community and sometimes share facilities within the community. Most of all, the local sports club should be seen as the first stepping stone towards international competitions.

National organisation of sport

AQA	✓
EDEXCEL	✗
OCR	✗
WJEC	✓
CCEA	✓

In order for their members to take part in competitions, local sports clubs need to have some sort of relationship with other clubs, either locally or nationally. Clubs achieve this by affiliating with the **National Governing Body (NGB)** of their sport.

Each sport in the UK has its own governing body, the main functions of which are to...

- establish and maintain the rules of the sport
- organise competition in the sport
- promote the sport
- select international teams for the sport.

Make sure you know the functions of NGBs.

A typical NGB is the Lawn Tennis Association (LTA) founded in 1888.

Figure 11.3 Responsibilities and duties of a National Governing Body

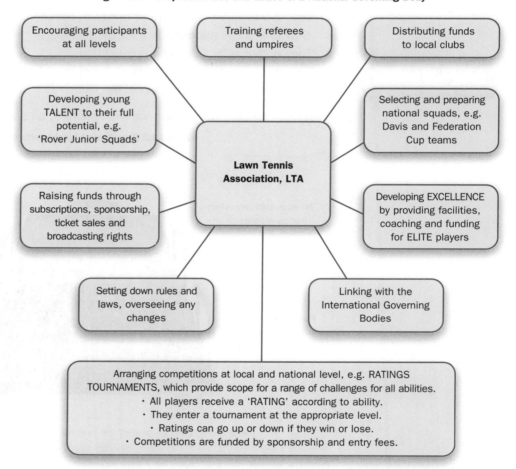

Some governing bodies have been in existence for a long time; others developed more recently (see Table 11.1).

Table 11.1 Establishment of some governing bodies of sport

Date	Club
1857	The Alpine Club
1871	The Rugby Football Union
1886	The Hockey Association
1949	The Basketball Association
1967	The British Orienteering Federation

To help promote their own and other sporting interests at a national level, the **NGBs** helped to set up the **Central Council for Physical Recreation (CCPR)**. The **CCPR** was established in 1935 with the express aim of representing the NGBs of sport. Today it acts as a voice for over 250 governing bodies. It is a **voluntary organisation** and is partly funded by the governing bodies. The main aims of the CCPR are to...

- promote the development of sport and physical recreation
- give support to specialist sports bodies
- develop award schemes
- act as a consultative body to the various Sports Councils and others concerned with sport.

> Make sure you know the aims of the CCPR.

The CCPR has established the **Sports Trust**, which runs the **Community Sports Leader Awards (CSLA)** for local leaders of sport. Extra funding for the CCPR comes from donations, sponsorship and grants from the **Sports Councils**.

> All lottery funding is allocated by UK distributors who manage their own grant programmes.

KEY POINT

Overall, the CCPR serves the NGBs of sport and passes on their views to the Sports Councils, central government and local authorities.

Figure 11.4 Basic framework of sport in the UK

> UK Sport works alongside Sport England, Sport Scotland, Sport Wales and Sport Northern Ireland.
>
> The IOC is not part of the UK sport framework, but is a key partner.

The original **Sports Council** was established by Royal Charter in 1972 and was funded by an annual grant from central government. The aims of the original Sports Council were to ensure that...

- all young people had the opportunity to acquire sports skills and physical education
- all adults had the opportunity to take part in the sport of their choice
- everyone had the opportunity to improve their standard in sport
- the moral and ethical basis of sport was maintained, and people were safeguarded from political, commercial and financial exploitation whilst involved with sport.

> You must be aware of this change in Sports Council organisation.

In 1996, however, the Sports Council was replaced by the **United Kingdom Sports Council (UK Sports Council)**, together with separate sports councils for each of the home countries: **Sport England**, **Sport Scotland**, **Sport Wales** and **Sport Northern Ireland**.

The primary functions of the UK Sports Councils are shown in Table 11.2.

Table 11.2 Functions of Sports Councils

The key roles of the Home Country Councils are to:	• Increase participation. • Improve the number and quality of facilities available. • Raise standards and develop excellence. • Allocate lottery funding.
The key roles of UK Sport are to:	• Support elite performers. • Oversee doping control, ethics and sports science. • Promote international status by attracting major events, e.g. world cups. • Co-ordinate all organisations within the national framework.

> You should be aware of the different spheres of influence of each of the Sports Councils.

Sport England is an organisation with offices in nine regions of England. Sport England manages a number of **national sports centres**, which help to develop elite talent as well as offering recreational opportunities.

Figure 11.5 National sports centres

The following sports centres are under the direction of Sport England:

- **Bisham Abbey** in Buckinghamshire provides for over 20 sports, including soccer, rugby, hockey and tennis.
- **Lilleshall** in Shropshire concentrates on gymnastics, cricket and football.
- **Holme Pierrepont** in Nottinghamshire concentrates on water sports activities.
- **EIS Sheffield** (English Institute of Sport) in South Yorkshire concentrates on indoor sports and athletics.

> Sport Wales, Sport Scotland and Sport Northern Ireland have their own national sports centres.

These sports centres are complemented by the **Manchester Velodrome** (the national cycling centre) and the **Crystal Palace** in South London, a multi-sports, athletics and swimming centre.

All these sports centres include top-flight training facilities, residential facilities and often host local, national and international events.

> It is a good idea to know who is the current Secretary of State for Culture, Media and Sport. (Keep checking as it does change.)

In modern day terms, the various sports councils are known as **quangos (quasi-autonomous non-governmental organisations)**. This means that although they were set up and financed by central government, they are not controlled by central government. They get their grant from the Department of Culture, Media and Sport, which is led by the Secretary of State for Culture, Media and Sport, and supported by the Minister for Sport.

Sport England has recently produced a radical new strategy to get more people playing sport. It aims to meet five targets by 2012:

1. To get one million more people playing sport
2. To reduce, by 25%, the drop-out rate from sport by people aged 16 and over
3. To improve talent development in at least 25 chosen sports
4. To increase people's satisfaction in playing sport
5. To contribute to the delivery of the 5-hour sports offer for young people

Raising standards

The structure of sport must assist in the development of elite performances. It must also recognise that there are few elite performers in a great number of participants (see Figure 11.6). The climb to the top of the pyramid requires the support of an established **national coaching process**. The establishment of **Sports Coach UK**, based in Leeds, produced a **UK Coaching Framework**, which aims to help performers get to the top of their chosen sport.

Figure 11.6 Sports pyramid

Figure 11.7 Coaching pyramid

Excellence / Performance / Participation / Foundation

Individual personal coach or trainer / National top level coaches / Advanced coaches / Teachers and club coaches / Family and friends

KEY POINT

Home and international affairs are looked after by different bodies.

International organisation of sport

AQA	✓
EDEXCEL	✗
OCR	✗
WJEC	✓
CCEA	✓

Some organisations are directed specifically to the organisation of international sport. These include the BOA, the IOC, the ISF and the BPA.

The British Olympic Association (BOA) organises the British Olympic team, known as 'Team GB'. The national governing bodies nominate their individual athletes, but they are selected and managed by the BOA at the Olympic Games. The BOA also initiates British bids to host the Olympic Games. Its most notable achievement has been its success in initiating the successful bid for the **2012 Olympic Games in London**.

Table 11.3 Key roles of the BOA

BOA **BRITISH OLYMPIC** ASSOCIATION	The key roles of the BOA are to... • select and manage the British team (Team GB) for the Olympic Games and organise their preparation and participation • be the strong independent voice for British Olympic sport • foster the Olympic ideals and movement • raise money without political involvement • promote participation at all levels.

The **International Olympic Committee (IOC)** is the ultimate authority on all matters relating to the Olympic Games. Its membership is drawn from national Olympic committees and **International Sports Federations (ISFs)**.

Table 11.4 Key roles of the IOC

IOC	The key roles of the IOC are to... • select venues, i.e. the host cities, and plan the games in conjunction with the hosts and ISF • approve the sports to take place in the games • promote sporting ethics, e.g. fair play, non-use of drugs • promote sport development and participation around the world • oppose political and commercial abuse.

The **International Sports Federation (ISF)** for each sport has the ultimate responsibility for all matters relating to that sport. Each national governing body of a sport has representation on that sport's ISF (see Figure 11.8).

Figure 11.8 Administration of sport to international level

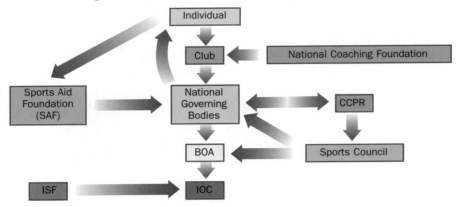

The **British Paralympic Association (BPA)** is responsible for selecting, preparing, entering, funding and managing Britain's team at the **Paralympics**. The Paralympics take place every four years in the same city and year as the summer and winter Olympic Games. They are elite multi-sport events that are a direct parallel to the Olympic Games. The BPA is supported by **Disability Sport England (DSE)** (formerly the British Sports Association for the Disabled) and the **English Federation of Disability Sport (EFDS)**, the national body responsible for developing sport for disabled people in England. It works closely with the five **National Disability Sports Organisations (NDSOs)**:

• **British Amputees and les Autres Sports Associations**
• **British Blind Sport**
• **Wheel Power – British Wheelchair Sport**
• **Mencap Sport**
• **UK Deaf Sport.**

Disability Sport Events

PROGRESS CHECK

1. Who are described as 'officers' of a local sports club?
2. What does NGB stand for and what are its four main functions?
3. What do the following stand for? **(a)** SAF **(b)** IOC **(c)** BOA **(d)** BPA?

1. President, secretary and treasurer. 2. National Governing Body. To establish and maintain rules; To organise competitions; To promote the sport; To select international teams. 3. (a) Sports Aid Foundation. (b) International Olympic Committee. (c) British Olympic Association. (d) British Paralympic Association.

11.3 Funding of sport

LEARNING SUMMARY

After studying this section you should be able to understand:
- how money is raised for sport
- how voluntary and professional clubs are financed

Raising money for sport

AQA	✓
EDEXCEL	✗
OCR	✗
WJEC	✓
CCEA	✓

All sportspeople will be aware of the need to generate sums of money so that sporting activities can take place. There are several ways in which this money can be obtained:

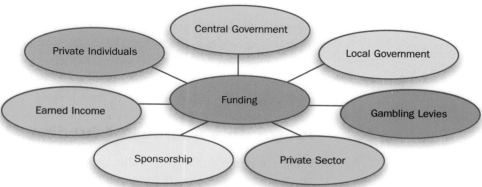

Central Government – the government does not put money directly into sport. It raises money through taxes paid directly by individuals and firms and indirectly through VAT on goods. From the revenue generated by taxes, it pays a grant to the Sports Councils for them to spend on sport. This was in the region of £45 million a year in the 1970s, but with 2012 in mind, Sport England has provided an investment of £480 million with the DCMS (Department of Culture, Media and Sport) pledging a further £1 billion towards the development of sports facilities.

> **KEY POINT**
>
> Central government does not own sports facilities or run sport – it is an enabling influence.

Local Government – local authorities raise their cash from council taxes and business tax. All this is spent on local services – schools, youth clubs and sports clubs, and very often on the provision of leisure centres, football pitches in parks and other sports facilities.

Gambling levies – these are often the main source of income for smaller clubs. Most small clubs hold raffles to raise funds. On a much bigger scale, the government charges a levy on all gambling including the **National Lottery (Lotto)**. This particular 'sweepstake' was established in 1994 with the aim of supporting a number of good causes, including sport. It is estimated that, for every £1 staked on the National Lottery, 28p goes to good causes, with 6p going to sport.

> You should be able to explain the various sources available for funding sport.

The National Lottery is a **primary source** of funding for the 2012 Games based in London and a greater share of the lottery monies is to be provided for sport over the next four years. Sport England directs lottery funds to sport through their NGBs.

Private sector – this type of finance comes in two specific ways:
- from developers who build private sports facilities and run them at a profit (many fitness clubs, gyms and golf clubs operate this way)
- from private companies making loans to clubs in exchange for some franchise operation (for example, many breweries make loans to clubs who agree to sell only their products).

Sponsorship – commerce, industry and local authorities are often prepared to invest in sport, a sports project or even an individual sportsperson. In exchange for a contribution of cash, or sometimes goods, the sponsor's name is associated with the sport and is on permanent display.

Earned income – the size of this must never be underestimated. Small clubs may charge fees for the use of their facilities and sell goods to their members or the public. Some larger clubs, such as football clubs, obtain a huge income from selling sports merchandise and replica kits.

Private individuals – some wealthy people can often be persuaded to invest money in sports clubs. A millionaire might buy his favourite football club, and make himself chairman. For example, Manchester City and Chelsea football clubs are owned by wealthy men. Others just donate smaller sums of money to the club of their choice because of their love of the sport.

Alternative sources of funding

There are numerous agencies that provide funding for specific aspects of sport. The following are some of the more well-known agencies:
- The **Foundation for Sports and the Arts** – uses income generated from football pools promotions, giving grants to a wide range of projects.
- **Sports Aid** – offers financial support for sportspersons aged 12–18 years.
- **Sportsmatch** – a grass-roots sponsorship incentive scheme, which looks to match commercial sponsorship.
- **Community Club Development Programme (CCDP)** – looks to enhance club facilities and increase local community participation. This programme is administered by the Department of Culture, Media and Sport.

Finance of clubs

AQA	✓
EDEXCEL	✓
OCR	X
WJEC	✓
CCEA	X

Amateur clubs

> **KEY POINT**
>
> Amateur clubs have lots of sources of income, although most are small.

Amateur sports clubs are run on quite small budgets. All the cash they get is spent on the members of the club (see Figure 11.9).

Figure 11.9 Amateur sports club wheel of wealth

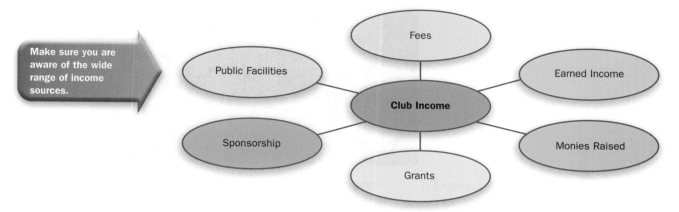

> Make sure you are aware of the wide range of income sources.

Fees – these form the basic income for some clubs. All members are required to pay a membership fee. Players often pay more than social members and young people often pay less than adults.

Earned income – most clubs attempt to sell merchandise (e.g. kit, items from the bar) to members and visitors. If the club plays matches at a high enough standard, it can charge admission fees to spectators. The selling of advertising space in match programmes and around the pitch also provides a useful income. Clubs with their own facilities may rent out their club house for functions or use their ground to raise extra income from car boot sales (see Figure 11.10).

Figure 11.10 A car boot sale at a rugby club in the off-season

Monies raised – many clubs charge members match fees every time they play in order to cover the cost of kit cleaning and repair. Most also organise raffles at specific times of the year and hold social events, such as dinners. These are expected to run at a profit for the club.

Grants – these can form a large part of the income of a small club. They may be available from the local authorities to pay for regular expenses, or from a Sports Council or National Lottery for bigger projects.

Figure 11.11 A voluntary club benefits from lottery cash with the support of the Sports Councils

Sponsorship – this might come at a local level from small businesses that have an interest in the sport, and may, therefore, mean that the kit has the sponsor's name on it.

Public facilities – although not a form of income for a club, facilities are often provided free of charge or at a reduced rate for sports clubs. The clubs benefit by saving money. Local authorities see this as providing a service to local people who are members of local clubs.

Professional clubs

Professional clubs often need to have a much greater income than amateur clubs, if they are to function properly. They have bigger outgoings than smaller clubs, especially as they have to pay wages and provide good facilities for spectators. They get their income from a number of sources (see Figure 11.12)

Figure 11.12 Professional sports club wheel of wealth

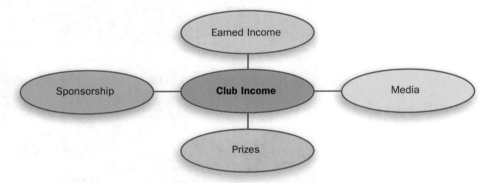

Remember that professional clubs are in business to make money.

> **KEY POINT**
>
> Professional clubs may have fewer sources of income, but the sources provide much larger sums of money.

Earned income – replica kits, sports merchandise, spectators' entry fees and advertising can all provide a large slice of income. (Clubs change strips regularly to maintain income.) The possible 'sale' of players also comes into this category.

Media – media organisations often pay large amounts of money to broadcast sports. Some professional clubs will have a regular contract either through their governing body or individually with radio or television, so that matches can be promoted and broadcast.

Prizes – in professional sports circles, not only can players earn large cash bonuses for winning popular competitions, but the clubs themselves may receive prize money.

Sponsorship – this and the endorsement of goods will provide a substantial income, especially for successful teams. Sponsors get a great deal out of sport: free advertising on players and around the ground, an improved image and often lots of hospitality from the clubs. The negative side of this is that sponsors only want to be associated with the successful clubs, those that have a big following or those that get a lot of media coverage. Loss of sponsorship cash can lead to less success on the pitch and a steady decline in support for the club.

> **PROGRESS CHECK**
>
> 1. How does central government give money to sport?
> 2. Which popular gambling activity provides large amounts of cash for sport?
> 3. List three ways in which an amateur club might earn income from sport.
>
> 1. Through an annual grant to the Sports Councils.
> 2. The National Lottery.
> 3. **Any suitable answers, e.g.** Selling goods; Renting out facilities; Car boot sales.

11.4 Providers of sport

LEARNING SUMMARY	**After studying this section you should be able to understand:**
	• the difference between private, public and voluntary provision
	• who national and local providers of facilities are
	• who voluntary and commercial providers of facilities are

Modes of provision

AQA	✓
EDEXCEL	✓
OCR	✓
WJEC	✓
CCEA	✓

The provision of sporting facilities can be divided into three main areas:
- **private** and **commercial**
- **public / local**
- **voluntary**.

Private and commercial facilities

Private and **commercial** clubs are provided by private monies for the benefit of people who wish to pay to use them. Although they are often run on a membership basis, this membership has to be paid for and the profits from the club go to the owners, not the members. If the clubs do not get enough members paying for their use, they soon go out of business. Examples of this type of private club are health centres, hotel swimming pools and holiday centres, such as Center Parcs and Haven.

There are two main types of commercial providers:
1. Some companies provide facilities for their employees – these include large commercial organisations such as banks or government departments. Although these facilities are in the commercial provision category, it is not the aim of the provider to make a profit. Employees are often asked to make a small donation towards the running cost of such facilities, but the bulk of their cost is borne by the company providing them. The main advantage of this type of provision is that employees, and often their guests, get sporting opportunities at a subsidised rate.

2 Some facilities are run on a profit-making basis – there is quite a wide range of this type of provision. Sport today is becoming a big industry and this is reflected in the growing number of private health clubs. Many cater only for specific sports and often charge large membership and entry fees. Only members and their guests can use them. Alongside these private clubs are enterprises such as fitness centres, bowling alleys and skating rinks.

Although most commercial providers are open to the public, they exist to make a profit. If they do not make a profit, private sports clubs and other sporting ventures will close down.

Do not overlook sports facilities in the holiday industry.

Public / local facilities

Public / local facilities are provided from the public purse and are open to all members of the public. A membership scheme might well exist but it is not restrictive; anybody can join. The main providers of public facilities are local councils that develop facilities for the benefit of the community as a whole. They do not have to run at a profit, but should not run at a substantial loss either. Examples of this type of facility are local sports centres, leisure centres and swimming pools.

Bear in mind that local councils see local provision as part of their civic duty.

Voluntary facilities

Voluntary facilities are provided by groups of people within a local community. They usually provide for a limited number of sporting activities, sometimes only one. They have a membership scheme – members usually run the club – and any profits made go back to the membership to spend on the club. They usually own or lease their facilities and are organised by the members, for the members. Examples of this type of provider are local sports clubs, the YHA and even a church hall that runs the occasional yoga class. Individuals are not restricted in their use of these facilities; they are all available to everybody (see Figure 11.13).

Note that voluntary facilities are usually small local clubs that have links with NGBs.

> **KEY POINT**
>
> All sports provision comes from the private, public or voluntary sectors.

Figure 11.13 Providers of sports facilities

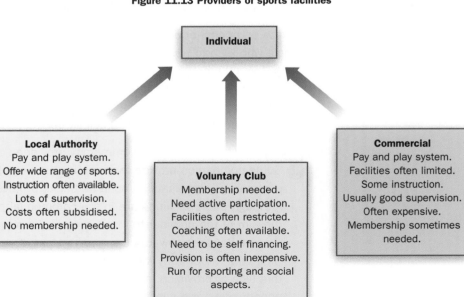

Individual

Local Authority
Pay and play system.
Offer wide range of sports.
Instruction often available.
Lots of supervision.
Costs often subsidised.
No membership needed.

Voluntary Club
Membership needed.
Need active participation.
Facilities often restricted.
Coaching often available.
Need to be self financing.
Provision is often inexpensive.
Run for sporting and social aspects.

Commercial
Pay and play system.
Facilities often limited.
Some instruction.
Usually good supervision.
Often expensive.
Membership sometimes needed.

National and local providers

The main providers of sport facilities at **national level** are the Sports Councils, National Governing Bodies (NGBs) and a number of specialist organisations such as **Natural England**, the **Forestry Commission**, and the **Environment Agency**:

- **Natural England** is a national organisation that provides local facilities such as country walks and bridleways for public use, and is responsible for the designation of **National Parks** and **Areas of Outstanding Natural Beauty (AONBs)**.
- The **Forestry Commission** manages over three million acres of forest lands, to which the public has access for walking and riding.
- The **Environment Agency** not only controls fishing on inland waterways but also caters for canoeing, boating, water-skiing and white-water rafting.

The main providers of facilities at a local level are local councils and voluntary clubs. Most local authorities have a department that is responsible for sport and leisure facilities, which will often work closely with a **Parks Department** that maintains the pitches, and an **Engineering Department** that maintains the heating plant in a swimming pool. Sports and leisure complexes are expensive to build and run, and often a local authority will develop such a facility in partnership with local industry and / or its national sports council.

> You should know about the contribution made by these national organisations.

> You should know what your local authority provides for sport.

Figure 11.14 Sport and leisure facilities provided

It is essential that these large types of facility include a wide range of sporting opportunities. They must offer indoor and outdoor sports, and changing facilities for all users. Indoor pools, sports halls, squash courts and outdoor fields provide for sporting activities, but a centre may also cater for community leisure activities. Halls can be used for concerts, displays and social events, and outdoor permanent play areas can be provided. To ensure the full use of these centres, adequate parking and local transport provision must be made.

Figure 11.15 Recreational facilities for the very young

A BVPP has built-in performance indicators, which are monitored.

Although the local authority may build a sports or leisure complex, the way it is run is directed by central government. Since April 2000, the authority must produce Best Value Performance Plans (BVPP), which show that the facilities are being run to a high standard. These plans provide for reduced rate or privileged admission charges for groups such as the young, senior citizens or the unemployed.

Many factors affect the location and development of a sports facility. These are often referred to as the '**6 Ps of influence**', and are major factors in the successful use of facilities (see Figure 11.16)

Figure 11.16 Factors affecting the location of facilities

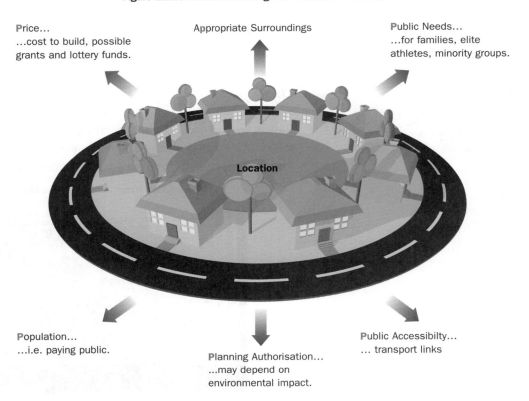

Price...
...cost to build, possible grants and lottery funds.

Appropriate Surroundings

Public Needs...
...for families, elite athletes, minority groups.

Location

Population...
...i.e. paying public.

Planning Authorisation...
...may depend on environmental impact.

Public Accessibilty...
... transport links

Voluntary providers

You must be able to describe what voluntary clubs are and why they exist.

Voluntary providers are clubs that provide sporting opportunities at a local level. They cater for the wide range of sporting interests that can be found in any local community.

Many of these clubs hire their facilities from the local authority. Few athletics clubs can afford to acquire their own all-weather running track. Others, however, are able to own and run their own premises. Very often such clubs get a regular financial grant from their local authority to help towards their running costs.

The main aim of these voluntary clubs is not to make a profit, but to provide sporting opportunities for local people at both a competitive and a recreational level.

PROGRESS CHECK

1. What type of provider is: **(a)** a local hockey club? **(b)** a sports centre?
2. Who are the two main providers of facilities at a local level?
3. Which type of commercial provider does not aim to make a profit?

3. Private facilities provided by companies for their employees.
2. Local authorities; Voluntary clubs.
1. **(a)** A voluntary provider. **(b)** A public provider.

Sample GCSE questions

1 Give **four** ways in which money is raised for sport through gambling.

National Lottery; Football pools; Betting levies on dog / horse racing; Raffles; Sweepstakes. **(4)**

> Only four answers are required, so any four of these would be acceptable. Make sure you are clear and specific in your answers.

2 Explain how amateur sports clubs are funded.

Membership fees - most clubs charge a yearly rate for membership.

Earned income, including sale of kit, refreshments, bar takings, admission charges and sale of advertising space around the pitch.

Grants - small grants from a local authority and larger ones from the sports council / National Lottery.

Sponsorship - usually from local business rather than national concerns.

Monies raised by raffles and social events - usually organised at specific times of the year, e.g. Christmas, summer. **(8)**

> A list is not enough – an explanation of each point you make is essential. There are 8 marks available, so you need to make at least 4 points, with a good explanation for each.

3 Explain how sponsors benefit from sponsorship deals.

Free advertising - the company name is put in front of many spectators and television viewers.

Improved status - winning teams suggest that the goods advertised are also winners, and that the goods have helped the team to win.

Hospitality - free tickets are provided to big games so that the sponsors can `show off´ and impress clients.

Improved image - by putting money into a charitable event, a company can appear to be caring rather than purely commercial. **(8)**

> Again, 8 marks are available, so you need to make at least 4 points and give an explanation for each point.

Exam practice questions

1 Explain how a local authority might help a local sports club financially.

....

....

....

.... **(4)**

2 Which sporting activities are included in the National Curriculum?

....

....

.... **(5)**

3 List **five** types of awards / exams, below degree level, which are offered in schools or colleges.

(a) ....

(b) ....

(c) ....

(d) ....

(e) .... **(5)**

4 Explain the terms **private provision** and **public provision**. Give one example of each type of provision.

....

....

....

....

.... **(10)**

Exam practice answers

Chapter 1 The major body systems

1. Femur.
2. (a)–(b) Any two from: Blood production; Protection; Support; Movement.
3. (a) Closing of a joint.
   (b) Opening of a joint.
   (c) Circular action.
4. Tough fibrous connective tissue joining two bones together. They strengthen and stabilise joints and limit movement in certain directions.
5. Smooth – found in walls of stomach / gut; Striated / striped / skeletal – found where muscles move bones; Cardiac – found in heart.

Chapter 2 Fitness

1. (a) (i) Time. (ii) Frequency. (iii) Type.
   (b) Progression.
   (c) Progression.
   (d) Reversibility.
   (e) Specificity.

Chapter 3 Training methods and programmes

1. Temperature regulation.
2. (a) High intensity work; (b) Low intensity work follows.
3. (a)–(b) In any order: Static; Ballistic.
4. (a) Training Threshold Rate.
   (b) Deduct age from 180, i.e. for a forty year old: 180 – 40 = 140 (TTR)
5. Any series of exercises where each exercise puts emphasis on a different body part, e.g. Shuttle runs to work the legs; sit-ups to work the abdominal muscles; press-ups to work the arms; star jumps to work the legs; back raiser to work the dorsal muscles and hamstrings; pull-ups to work the arms.

Chapter 4 Skill

1. The speed at which a decision is made.
2. (a)–(b) Any two suitable sports, for example: Boxing; Judo; Tennis.
3. The learned ability to bring about pre-determined results with maximum certainty, with minimum outlay of time, energy, or both.
4. Sensory: carry information to the CNS. Effector: carry information away from the CNS.
5. (a)

Only a limited amount allowed through

Input from lots of sources → PERCEPTUAL PROCESS → DECISION MAKING

(b) They are prevented from being involved in the decision-making process.

Chapter 5 Measurement in sport

1. Suppleness.
2. Any suitable aspect, for example: Strength; Suppleness; Speed; Skill.

3. Muscular strength is immediate, short term. Muscular endurance is over a prolonged period of time.
4. (a) Cardiovascular fitness.
   (b) The subject steps fully onto and off a bench, 45cm high, for a period of five minutes at a rate of 30 steps per minute. After a one minute rest pulse rate is taken then doubled.
5. (a) Stork stand test.
   (b) The subject stands on one foot and places the other against the inside of the knee with hands placed on hips. Timing starts when both eyes are closed. Timing stops when eyes open, foot parts from knee or the subject loses balance.

Chapter 6 Factors affecting performance

1. Vitamins; Minerals; Fibre / roughage; Water.
2. (a) Carbohydrates.
   (b) Carbohydrates / fats.
   (c) Fats.
   (d) Fats / carbohydrates.
3. (a) Mesomorph.
   (b) Ectomorph.
   (c) Mesomorph.
   (d) Mesomorph / Ectomorph.
4. World Anti-Doping Agency. Its ultimate goal is for all athletes to benefit from the same anti-doping procedures.

Chapter 7 Safety in sport

1. Any one from: Break; Fracture; Strain; Torn ligament; Torn tendon.
2. Soft tissue injuries occur to muscles, tendons and ligaments; Hard tissue injuries occur to bones.
3. Legs.
4. Painted lines.
5. Any four from: Bend knees; Keep arms straight; Keep the load close to the body; Keep back straight; Lift using large muscle groups; Keep head up; Do not try to lift above head height.
6. Chronic back ache and damage to joints (arthritic conditions).

Chapter 8 Sport today

1. Concessionary entry for the young or non wage earners, restricted entry for women only or mothers and toddlers, minority provision for less popular sports, crèche facilities so mothers can take part on their own, courses for students during school holidays.
2. (a) May restrict joining an activity, may not be able to afford equipment, may not be able to partake in related social aspects of activity.
   (b) May restrict provision of less popular sports, can demand an unfair share of time, may only provide for a definitive part of the community, can exclude minority groups.
3. Any four from: Increase in number of bank holidays; Increase in amount of paid holidays; Shorter working week; Shorter working life; People live longer in retirement; More labour-saving goods; Faster transport.
4. (a) True
   (b) True
   (c) False
   (d) True
   (e) True
   (f) False.

Exam practice answers

Chapter 9 Participation

1. Inclusion of events for the disabled in main calendar of Games, recognition of categories for participation, development of Paralympic Games.
2. 1968 – Mexico City: black US athletes in Black Power salute, South Africa refused admission. 1972 – Munich: terrorists massacre Israeli team members.
3. Over-aggression, cheating, sledging.
4. Removal of perimeter fences, segregation of fans, all-seater stadia, use of CCTV inside and outside grounds, control of sale of alcohol, police forces sharing intelligence.

Chapter 10 Media and sponsorship

1. **Any one from:** Makes a product seem successful; Role models attract a following; Clean image of sportsperson reflects on product.
2. **(a)–(b) Any two from:** Change ruling of officials; Undermine officials; Can make decision for officials; Can educate or clarify a situation.
3. **(a)–(c) Any three from:** Better coverage of sport; Better analysis of sport; Create feedback for participants; Increased audience size; Improved safety; Improved standard of officiating.
4. Recipients: a sport, a team, an event, a competition, an individual. Types: money, kit / equipment, travel, scholarships, food.

Chapter 11 Organisation and provision of sport

1. Financial grants, grants in kind, reduced rates, provision of facilities.
2. Games, gymnastics, athletics, dance, swimming.
3. **(a)–(e) Any five from:** Sports achievement awards; Leaders courses; CSLA; GCSE courses; A Level courses; BTEC courses; GNVQ vocational courses.
4. Private – clubs, gyms, fitness centres, for members only use, run to make a profit.
   Public – local sports clubs run by the members for the members, local sports centres run by the local council, all non-profit making.

Index

Index